Situations 101

The real measure of your wealth,
Is how much you'd be worth if you lost
All of your money.

Situations 101

The real measure of your wealth,
Is how much you'd be worth if you lost
All of your money.

Bern Nadette Stanis

Worthingham Publishing

Published by:
Worthingham Publishing
8306 Wilshire Blvd.
Suite 303
Beverly Hills, CA 90211

Interior Design by:
Daniel-Melton Media, Inc.
17117 Westheimer Rd.
Suite 75
Houston, Texas 77082

ISBN: 978-0-9770361-2-7

Printed and bound in the United States of America
by Sumi Print and Finishing Solutions
http://www.getsumiprinting.com • 310-769-1600

Bern Nadette Stanis

Dedication

With All My Love

To My Mother Eula

My Daughters

Dior Ravel And Brittany Rose Cole

How Many Times

And

How Many Ways

Can I Simply Say

Undoubtedly,

Absolutely, Adoringly

And

Forever

"I Love You"

And

To My Family Everywhere

Especially I Thank God

For Giving Me The Vision For This Book

Acknowledgments

Trent T. Daniel

wishes to thank

My Sweet Diva Baby, Sarah Marie

My Babies
Dessiah, Sydney And Kira
My Loving Family
Joanne (The Original Risk Taker)

Fred Williams (Editor)

Margie Walker
Janet G. Balfour
Michael and Jacquelyn Emmers

Special Thanks to
David W. Hollins, Sr.
For Financial Information Used In This Book

and
Ms. Bern Nadette Stanis

Thank You

"When A Man Dreams"
A Poem to President Barack Obama

When a man dreams, he sees the desires in his heart and mind,
Dancing before him.
Here is where he's free to be all that he knows he can.
When a man dreams, he stands in the gap of where he's been
And where he knows he must be.
The Trojan, The Leader, The Preacher, The One.
When a man dreams, the beauty is there for him to see,
His children, male or female are his extension of his Legacy.

When a man dreams, his Woman, his Wife, The Mother of all,
Is the best part of him, it's his Freedom, his soil.
When a man dreams, he sees the truth of how it should be
Without demented perceptions of anything Ugly.
When a man dreams, he sees the World as his Home,
There are no boundaries, no limitations connected with fear.
No colors, No blacks and whites or shades stop here.

When a man dreams, he goes beyond the color of skin or
The finances one is encased in.
It's his spirit that soars, expressing the God within.
And, he knows he must reach to the end of the earth
For his friend.

continued

This can only be when a man is driven to Dream.
Like other men who have dreamt, The Dream.
Like Malcolm and Martin and so many in between.
Yes
This is what becomes of a man who dreams

The Leader, The Beacon, The One who must
Carry the Burden of Hope for all of US.
Yes
We must do our part and allow him to be
The one who must change
The Way Things Were.
Yes
We must do our part and allow him to be
The one who will,
Bridge Our World To Harmony.
And if we do our part and allow him to be
Barack Hussein Obama
President of The United States of America
Yes
Then we all will see, This one chart a brand new course
In Our World and In Our History.
Remember, This can only be,

"When A Man Dreams"

Bern Nadette Stanis

Table of Contents

Resource Center

Situation

1 Stretching That Dollar

I am spending an awful lot of money, and not on frivolous things, but those of importance. It seems like everyone is gouging you for money. I am the type of person that keeps a record of everything I spend. I review the receipts that I keep in a Ziplock bag every evening, so I know where every penny goes.

Recently, I have been spending a lot on food. It's not that I'm buying more, just spending more. I have budgeted and budgeted, and it still seems like I am spending more than I like. But I am buying what my family needs. Is there something else I can do? Can you suggest some ways to help me stretch my money a little further?

Response

I have heard this so often. People are spending more and getting less these days. The fact that you know where your money goes is a very good sign. Many people spend and don't watch what they spend their money on. That is the easiest way for a person to throw money away. When you keep records, you will know where you spend and how much you are spending. This will allow you to make adjustments. You can decide what is necessary to have versus what is waste.

There are some things you can start doing. Where do you shop for food? If you shop at large stores, such as a Wal-Mart, you can get name brand labels, sold at some of the higher end food chains, for a lot less. Sometimes, running into your corner store to buy something will be priced higher than it should be. This small adjustment may not seem like much at first, but over a year, you will be able to see the savings. You can put the money you're saving toward paying more than the minimum payment on your credit card, paying additional principle on your mortgage, or even putting it into your savings. Sometimes, small changes here and there make a big difference later. Try it. I'm sure you will see your money buy more for you.

Situation

2 My Children Need A Home

I am a single mother of two children. My son is 12 years old, and my daughter 10. I have been raising my children alone for three years. Before my husband and I divorced, we were trying to save for a house. We managed to save a decent sum in the eight years we were married. But when it became apparent things were not going to work out, all the money went out the window. It was used for everything else when we got the divorce. It was sad, but I still have the dream of providing a home for my children.

I've always believed that if you provide a comfortable environment for your children when they are teenagers, they will be able to bring their friends over and enjoy entertaining at home. I want to know my children's friends. That way, I will know where they are and what they are doing.

Can you give me some pointers on how I can save enough money for a decent down payment?

Response

That is a very interesting concept you have about your children staying at home to entertain. Although nothing is guaranteed, I do see your point. Getting back to saving for a down payment, ideally, you would like to be able to save up to 20%. That might not be so easy these days. Even with a home priced at two hundred thousand dollars, you are looking at coming up with 40-thousand. Look at it this way, if you do come up with a substantial down payment, you have instant equity in your home, which can be valuable down the road when or if you decide to sell. Don't let the 20% rule keep you from owning a home. You may even find the home of your dreams and save money with a smaller down payment.

There are sources that you can seek out when you begin to plan for the purchase of your home. Typically, the down payment will come from cash savings, but there are other options available. Check with the Federal Housing Administration or Veterans Administration, as well as state housing authorities for programs that can assist first time and low-to-moderate income families to obtain a mortgage with a low down payment. The US Department of Agriculture's Rural Housing Service also offers a program intended to encourage low-to-moderate income buyers to purchase in rural areas.

If you currently have money saved up in a retirement account, then there may be additional sources available to you. Some 401k retirement plans allow participants to borrow money from the account for a new home purchase. Also, if you have an IRA account, there are provisions to allow withdrawals for first time home purchases. A point to keep in mind is that money sitting in a savings account, earning less than one percent interest won't do much in helping you reach your savings goal faster. You want to make sure your money is working for you. If your plan is to purchase a home within the next few years, you may want to consider a high yield savings or money market account for holding the down payment fund.

I hope you find these pointers helpful. I also hope you find the perfect home that your children will love and enjoy. The best to you and this time, I hope your down payment will go to just that – the down payment for your new home.

Situation

3 Who Can I Trust?
(Hiring a Financial Planner)

I am not a spendthrift. I don't blow my money, and my favorite place for it is in the bank. I know it's safe there, even though I concede nothing's for sure these days. Still I believe the bank is the best place for my hard-earned money. I am a trucker. I've had my own truck for six years. Because I travel across the country all the time, I am still single at 38 years old. However, I am not looking to get married any time soon. I enjoy my work and my travels.

Recently, my parents made a decision to sell some property, and they gave me $145,000 from the proceeds of the sale. I deposited it straight away in the bank. I know it's time to have a professional help me set things up properly and manage my money well. I am looking for a financial advisor, but I am nervous about this because it's just so hard to know whom to trust. With the volatile things going on in the stock market and with these shady financial management firms, I am just nervous about hiring the wrong person for the job.

What should I look for in the process of hiring a financial advisor?

Response

It is refreshing to hear from someone who really enjoys what he is doing for a living. Now, about hiring a financial advisor. When it comes to hiring someone to manage your money, initially you are always going to be a little apprehensive because you are putting your money in someone else's hands. We have all heard horror stories about financial advisors taking advantage of their clients' money, causing them great loss.

These are some of the precautions you can take. Make sure that you interview several candidates before making a final decision. Request a list of clients from the candidates to ascertain whether they were satisfied with the financial manager's performance. You may also want to do a background check. It could help when making the final decision on who should manage your money.

I commend you for realizing that you need someone to help you manage your money. Making a decision to hire a financial advisor is one that should be taken very seriously. Good luck. I hope you find the right person to trust.

Situation

4 No Money To Tithe

Don't think I am a bad person or anything, because I'm not. My wife has been trying to get me to her church for years, but I have never gone. I pray right here at home. My problem is giving money to the church. I am a hard worker, and when I get my money, I have bills and expenses and there isn't a whole lot left. If I give to the church, I may not be able to give my children something they need. I might come up short. The preachers have money, and their children are doing well. I just can't see it any other way.

Recently, my wife and I had a big argument about her tithing every week. I told her that if we could save the money she is giving to the church, maybe we would have something one day. We don't see eye-to-eye. Because my hours have been cut back at work, things are even tighter now. My wife is still giving away our little money to the church. Who is she trying to impress?

Response

Have you ever heard that giving is essential to financial success? Give, and it shall be given unto you; good measure, pressed down and shaken together, and running over, shall men give unto your bosom. For with the same measure that you give, it shall be given back to you. (Luke 6: 38).

It would really help you understand the principle of tithing if you will just take the time and read about it in the bible. It really is not about you giving to the preacher. Tithing is a reminder to Jesus and you of the intent in your heart. There are many blessings when you tithe. It seems as if this is bothering you in some way, suggesting to me that you are looking for an answer. You can find the answer as to why one tithes. Not only will you find the answer in the bible, but you will find the answer in your heart. It must come from within. Your gifts must be pure of heart, not grudgingly, because God loves a cheerful giver. God is able to make all grace abounds toward you that you always have all sufficiency in all things, may abound to every good work: (Corinthians 2, 9:6-8).

Just give it a chance and see for yourself. I really hope that your wife and you can find peace in your home, that she can be patience with you, and maybe you will see things her way.

Situation

5 Pre-Approved Does Not Mean Approved

I don't have many credit cards so when I received this pre-approved credit card offer in the mail, with a line of credit worth $5,000, I was excited. I followed the instructions, filled out every blank line, and then sent it back to them.

A few weeks later, I got a letter from the credit card company saying that my recent application was denied. So, why did they send me the pre-approved card when they were not going to give me a card? This is terrible because people think one thing when it's not like that at all.

I really thought I was going to get that credit card. Why do they do this?

Response

It is sort of a trick. The credit card company was tricking you into applying for credit. It is a tactic credit card companies' use, and many people fall for it - just like you did.

When a credit card offer is sent to you declaring that you have been pre-approved, read the fine print. It will clearly tell you that you were not necessarily approved for a credit line, but you were pre-approved to receive an offer. The best thing to remember is that pre-approved does not mean approved. If a credit card company tells you that you were pre-approved, while simultaneously asking for information, it is not likely that a credit line has already been established for you.

There have been a number of laws that have come out in the last several years limiting this practice by credit card companies, but it is still happening. My best advice is to put any pre-approved credit offers you receive in the trash. If your credit is good enough to receive an approval from a credit card company, you will not need to respond to an offer that comes by mail.

Situation

6 I Don't Need Identity Theft Protection

I have been told to protect myself from identity theft. My friends always tell me,

"Girl, don't buy anything with your credit card on the Internet because someone can get your banking information and use your card."

I see television ads telling people to pay $10 a month to protect their identity. The warning rings in my ears, but what people don't know is that if a thief steals my identity, the joke's on them because my credit is so bad they will get absolutely nothing. So, identity theft is something I just don't worry about.

I have never had any problems, but my cousin had a serious problem. She was recently pulled over for speeding. When the police ran her driver's license, they came back to her and said, "There is a warrant for your arrest." She was certainly surprised.

When she went to court, she was told that a panhandler was begging for money in front of a business. The business owner called the police, and when the police asked the panhandler her name, she gave them my cousin's name. Instead of making sure the woman was who she said she was, the police just wrote the name she gave them. That's how my cousin got mixed up in all that mess. She finally got it straightened out, but now has to drive with a paper in the car from the court, stating that her identity was stolen.

That incident scared me, but I'm not sure how much getting identity protection will help. Do I still need to purchase the protection, even with my credit the way it is?

Response

It is important to understand that identity theft can affect you - even if you have bad credit. When it comes to identity theft, it is possible for your identity to be used in ways that you do not expect. What happened to your cousin is a prime example.

Another unsavory situation is when someone takes your information and opens a checking account in your name. If that person writes a check for more money than you have in your account, it will be reported to authorities. That company or entity will then send a letter to the address printed on the check, demanding payment for the bad check. If the letter is not answered, a warrant can be issued for your arrest. If you do not have identity theft protection, and you are arrested for a bad check, you are going to incur costs for legal fees that you will have to pay. In some cases, identity theft protection programs can help you in the process of clearing your name and potentially cover some of the costs associated with this process.

While this is just an example of how someone can abuse your identity, it is only one of many things that can happen. My advice to you is to make the investment and set up an identity theft protection program for your family members and you. While you can never know what will happen, you should always be prepared for the worst. Good credit or bad credit, everyone needs protection.

Situation

7 There Are No Quick Fix Solutions!
(To Fixing Your Credit)

I have been suffering with bad credit for a number of years now, and I am looking for a solution to help me with my bad credit situation. I am so far under that my credit will not be cleaned up for at least five years or more. I am paying a little at a time on the bills that I still owe.

One day I was on the Internet looking for that solution and I came across an interesting website. The sponsors of the site were saying that I could create another number to use in place of my social security number, when I apply for credit. According to the site, this number would allow me to create a new credit profile to get me approved for credit and that the bad credit on my profile would not show up.

This sounds like a great solution, but I'm wondering if this is something that could get me into trouble.

Response

If something sounds too good to be true, often times, it generally is.

Let me explain the number they are referring to in that interesting website you stumbled across. It is called a Credit Protection Number or CPN. The purpose of this number is to create a separate credit profile with the credit bureau that you can use to apply for credit.

The answer to your question is YES, it could get you into trouble. When a credit application requests your social security number and you put a different number on that application, then you are not telling the truth. It is against the law to lie on a credit application. While it is not illegal to have a credit protection number, it is illegal to misrepresent your social security number when applying for credit.

It is not clear as to how many people have actually gotten into trouble by using these credit protection numbers, but you do not want to be one of them. There are many sites on the Internet that prey on people who are trying to get approved for credit. My advice to you is do not try something that involves being dishonest or making statements that do not represent the absolute truth.

Not being able to get approved for credit is unfortunate, but getting approved for credit and getting into legal trouble will be a lot worse.

Situation

8 It's Time To Move
(Banks vs. Credit Unions)

Recently, I have run into a problem with my bank. It seems as if there are more and more fees and charges for this and that on my monthly statement. I mentioned my dissatisfaction with my bank to my brother. He suggested I do what he has always done - join a credit union, instead of using a bank. My brother has been telling me about credit unions for a while. I always said, "You know, I've been with the bank for years, and that's where I'll stay."

But I've noticed more and more little annoyances than I need right now. I even argued with my bank for treating me as if they don't know me, or as if I were a new customer. I don't care to go into all of the details about the situations I've run into with them, but I'm sure many people understand my position.

I know about banks, but I don't know much about credit unions. I do have a credit union at my job. Could you shed a little light on the differences between a bank and a credit union for me?

Response

Yes, I can tell you the difference. I will say first, however, dissatisfaction with the way some banks handle their customers is on the increase. That's true even for those who have been with their bank a long time. Sometimes, bankers treat you as if you are a stranger to their institution. Understandably, many people get very annoyed by this.

Speaking of the differences between a bank and a credit union, in the latter, you are considered part owner. Consequently, you are seen as a vital part of the growth of the enterprise and not just another customer. Another difference is that credit unions are non-profit organizations; therefore, interest rates and fees are usually much lower than commercial banks. Credit unions distribute dividends to their members, which means you are actually investing in yourself. Additionally, credit cards from credit unions usually have lower or no annual fees, and most credit unions offer free checking accounts. Incidentally, overdraft fees are usually a fraction of what the commercial banks charge.

So it definitely looks like credit unions can offer you more of the benefits you seem to be looking for. But before you make a final decision, be sure to compare the two in relationship to what truly makes you feel most comfortable. Think about the reason you never moved from the bank before. If the reason does not outweigh the benefits of the credit union, then it is a good idea to make the change.

Whichever you decide, I hope you will get the respect you deserve, and you won't have to put up with any more annoyances. Good luck.

Situation

9 I Should Have A Credit Card

(Credit Card Conflict)

Being 21 years old and a senior in college, I consider myself a responsible adult. I have a decent job working here at my school part time. My Mom is still making sure I am comfortable and takes care of some of my needs. She wants me to work and save and save and save. I do save, but I spend half of my check on clothes, hair stuff, and personal items.

The other day I received a credit card application in the mail. I thought maybe it would be cool to have a credit card for emergencies. My Mom doesn't agree. She says I have all of the money I need right now. What do you think?

Response

I see your point thinking you need a credit card for emergencies, but you have been doing well so far without one. I am in agreement with your Mom. I would advise you to stay away from credit cards while you are in college.

When you have a credit card, it seems like emergencies always come up. If not emergencies, then some other reason to use it will pop up. It might be to put gas in your car or gas in a friend's car. It might be to buy books or something extra you wouldn't normally buy if you didn't have the card. What is important to remember as a college student is that you may not be able to afford the interest rates that credit card companies charge for even those small purchases. If you have money coming in, you don't want to put yourself in a position to pay more for the money than what it is worth.

Let me give you an example of someone I knew who was in college. He had his first credit card and thought it would be so easy to make that minimum payment. Right? Wrong! What he didn't understand was that the more payments he made, the more his credit limits went up and therefore, the more he spent. His card payment started out as low as $15 a month grew to $35 a month, and before he knew it, his monthly bill was $150 a month. He began to panic. He couldn't afford to make his monthly payment. He couldn't believe how he went from a very small credit card bill he knew he could handle every month, to borrowing money from friends and his parents in order to keep up with his $150 monthly payment.

See how a simple dream credit card in college can turn into a nightmare payment later? Take my advice while you are in college. Please, just leave the credit cards alone. If you can't pay cash for it, then maybe you just don't need it. If you follow this simple but disciplined advice, it will keep you from making mistakes that will damage your credit and put you in a bad financial position for a long time.

Although you are an adult and it's your decision to make, it wouldn't hurt to listen to Mom on this one.

Situation

10 I Am Not A Deadbeat!
(I Want To Pay My Bills)

I am a nurse. I make a decent living, but I've been having some difficulties lately. I find that at the end of every month, I barely have enough money to live on after paying my bills. I am not an extravagant person and have always tried to live within my means.

Recently, due to some unfortunate issues, I have run into some problems. I had to cut down my hours at work at the hospital in order to help take care of my father. Because of this change, I am struggling emotionally, as well as financially.

I know that I am not a deadbeat, and this is not my fault, but I feel like I am sinking in quicksand. Although this is temporary and I am going to get more help for my dad, I am having trouble dealing with feelings of inadequacy and disappointment in my financial position at this point in my life. Everything is out of focus for me now. I just don't know where to start.

Response

Wow! I am sorry to hear about the trouble you are

facing, but you are like so many Americans going through similar experiences these days. That's why I say don't allow yourself to be one of those people who feel that not being able to pay bills on time is a direct reflection on who they are as a person. Look at what you are doing for your father! You are there for him. So many people would just put their parent in a nursing home. Taking care of your father is saying a lot for your character. You should be proud. I am sure you are a wonderful person, so please be patient with yourself. Don't associate your personal self-worth or self-esteem with your ability to pay bills or not pay bills.

I understand that the problem you are having financially is not because you are not working hard. It is because you are not making enough money. I would suggest that you come up with other ways to create more money for yourself, something you can do outside of your job. It doesn't have to be complicated, but something simple. Think about the things you enjoy doing. Think about something you're passionate about. There are so many businesses that can be created from doing something we love to do. Ultimately, you would be doing something that would make you very happy, and if you can create a business from it, you will have more money, too.

Situation

11 They Stress Me Out!

(Collection Agents)

The phone rings non-stop these days. All of the calls seem to come from collection agencies. My husband and I have fallen on hard times. Although we have tried everything short of anything illegal, we are behind in our bills. I have tried to make arrangements with the companies that we owe money to, but even when I manage to make arrangements, I can't keep up.

Now the collection agencies are calling with no end in sight. I am on edge and stressed out. My husband has the attitude that if we don't have the money where do they think we are going to get it from, so he really doesn't let it bother him like I do.

The other day I answered one of their calls, thinking maybe I can reason with these people. The person on the other end was so unreasonable, I panicked. He said because of my delinquent payment, I was as good as a thief and that my husband and I were in trouble. He said the police were on their way to serve an arrest warrant on us.

That day felt like hell to me. Scared to death, I left the house. My husband was not home. I went to one of my friend's house. She could tell I was upset. I didn't want to tell her my business, but I really didn't know what to do. So I told her what happened, and she said that was one of the tactics they use to put fear into people. Oh, my goodness! That is terrible for anyone to do that. It could cause people who don't understand their tactics to panic and anything could happen. Well, my husband and I did not have a warrant for our arrest.

How can these people be stopped? What can we do?

Response

There is certainly something that can be done. This is a very common occurrence, and while it may seem to get results for some collection agencies that resort to these tactics, it is illegal for them to do this.

I have heard stories such as yours, but the people who were told these things from the collection agency were not as lucky as you were. They did not have someone who could tell them that the agency was lying in order to scare them into paying their bills. A few of them ended up hurting themselves, and a few ended up causing accidents and hurting other people.

There is the Fair Debt Collections Practices Act, which is a federal law that was created to regulate collection agencies. That law is very powerful, but most consumers do not know about it; therefore, they do not exercise their rights.

Anyone trapped in a position where the collection agencies are calling excessively should remember some rules. Here are a few of them.

1. There is a certain time frame in which the debt collector can contact you, regarding your debt. You may be contacted between the hours of 8AM and 9PM. Any calls made outside of those times, as well as the times you specifically told them are inconvenient for you, is a violation of this rule.

2. Use of foul language, profanity of any form, or any verbal abuse by the debt collection agency is strictly prohibited. They are not allowed to threaten you in any verbal or physical way, including the threat to publicize your debt or tell your superior about the debt you have incurred, which may threaten the job or the jobs that you have.

3. The debt agency is not allowed to file legal action in a place that is not near the creditor's home. A case should be filed in your state.

4. The law states that the collection agency cannot contact any third party regarding the debt that you owe without your consent. In some cases where contact information does not exist, the credit agency is allowed one phone call to find

the debtor, but they are not allowed to divulge that they are calling regarding credit collection.

I really wish you knew about this law that protects you from abusive debt collectors before you had to go through what you did. Now that you know, tell as many of your friends as you can. You never know who may need to know about it.

I hope the finances get better for you and your husband, so that you can take care of all of your bills and you won't need to ever hear from those agencies again. Not ever.

Situation

12 Only $50 Of That Is Principal

(Paying My Mortgage Off)

On the heels of a new marriage, my husband and I recently bought our first home. We both are fortunate to have parents that can help us financially, which includes supporting us financially in our own business. We want to pay off our home early. We currently have 24 years left on our mortgage. If we can pay it off in the next 10 years, we will purchase another home. The one we are in now will become an investment property for us.

Our house payment is $2,000 a month. Only fifty dollars of that is principle, and the rest is interest. So, if we paid $1,950.00 on one check for interest and paid $600 on another check for principle, would that knock a full year off the payment term?

Response

That is exactly right. It is possible to cut the term of your mortgage just by paying your principal and interest payments separately and by applying more money toward principle payments each month. When you buy a home, the first year of your mortgage payments are applied mostly to interest. The company that is financing your home should have supplied you with something called an amortization schedule. That schedule is a list of all the payments you will be making on your home, with a breakdown of how much goes to principle and how much to interest. If you look at that schedule, you will see that the majority of your payments initially are going to be applied toward the cost of the money, as opposed to the actual money borrowed.

The practice of paying more on your mortgage every month is very smart because it is going to help you eliminate your mortgage in a shorter time period. When you send in the payment, always specify the additional amount is to be applied to principal. Otherwise, the mortgage company will apply it as a partial payment towards your next months mortgage. The best way to handle these payments is to write two separate checks - one for the principal and one for the interest every month. That way there is no misunderstanding about where the payments should be applied.

I am proud of you and your husband for working together the way that you are. When couples work this way, they can achieve wonderful rewards in their lifetime. Happiness and success to you both.

Situation

13 My Little Tea Shop
(SBA Loans)

My sister and I opened a little teashop in a quaint area of town. The location is close to a college campus and has done us well. We are open from 11AM to 11PM. The long hours have been hard on us, but the business is great.

The customers that come in are college students. They work on their course assignments, get on their computers, and some come in simply to absorb the atmosphere and text all night. We offer teas from all over the world, as well as different cakes and cookies. It's like a big family, as every one seems to know each other. The shop is small, with a few couches, but it is time for us to expand.

The owner has mentioned to us that he would like to sell the building. He asked if we were interested in buying it. The benefit is that we would be able to expand our teashop into a full-blown eatery with the additional square footage. We would add sandwiches, salads, and coffee to the menu. We used our own personal money to start our business. My sister and I have survived off the sales from this business only for two years now. We can see it growing but we need a loan to expand. This is our dream.

Can you explain what we need to do so we can get a decent loan for our expansion?

Response

Look into a lender that specializes in SBA loans that focus on developing small businesses that are accountable, accessible, and responsible. An SBA loan can work well for your enterprise. They are loans with a good interest rate and backed by the federal government. This means that if you are approved for one, the federal government will back the loan in case you default. Consequently, SBA loans require good credit. An applicant should have been in business for at least two to three years. The applicant also has to produce good financial records. You must show profitability for those two or three years as proof to the lender that you have the ability to repay the loan.

They also want to see that you are hiring new employees with your expansion. Minority employees are a plus. I am sure that if your sister and you meet all of these requirements, you will get the loan, be able to purchase the building and see your dream come true.

Situation

14 Everyone Can Save
(Emergency Funds)

I am a single woman living alone. I am a receptionist; therefore, I must watch how I spend my money. My concern is that I don't have money to put away for emergencies. This is the frightening aspect of being alone. There is usually no one to fall back on. I have a car note, rent, lights, gas and food. Occasionally, I spend a little on something new to wear. I have a couple of male friends that I see here and there, but no one I can say is that special person. I like living alone and not having to answer to anyone. I only get lonely when I am by myself on holidays or my birthday. It has happened a few times. I know this makes me sound paranoid, but what if I get sick and have to go to the hospital? What if I need a few hundred dollars for some other emergency? This is what scares me the most. I don't make a lot of money, so how can I have an emergency fund?

Response

Having an emergency fund is not an impossible task to accomplish. In your case, I would stop focusing on all that you don't have and instead, look at what you do have. If you could save $5 a day for five (5) days a week, you would have $25 in one week. In one month, you would have $100. If you maintain this routine, you would have $1200 saved up in one year! I think that is a good start. Whatever money you don't use in one year, carry it over to the next.

Just remember, you don't always need a lot of money to save money. You can start with a little and work up from there. With consistency and dedication, you'd be surprised at how every little bit adds up. See now, you too, can have an emergency fund.

Situation

15 Look Before You Leap
(Power of Attorney)

There is something that bothers me. About five months ago, I met this attorney and his wife at a banquet I attended for my business. I explained to the attorney that I needed legal counseling and wanted to get into investing. He seemed like a decent person and a good attorney.

I own a boutique that carries designer clothes. I am doing very well, so this is why I need an attorney to help me with some of my business ideas. I had a few meetings with him and all went well. At the last meeting, he suggested I give him power of attorney. I asked him why. He replied that because I am so busy, there are times when he can't get in touch with me whenever he needs to. With the power of attorney, he can take care of things on a timely basis. I never got back to him on this, but he is persistent on getting this done. He calls and leaves messages for me to let him know if this is something I want to do.

Before I return his calls, I need to inquire more about this. I assume a power of attorney can benefit my situation, as I am very busy. Except for the two girls who work in the boutique, I handle every aspect of my business alone. I need counsel about the counsel.

Can you tell me whether or not I should give him power of attorney?

Response

I don't know if you are aware of it, but there are different types of power of attorney. Did your attorney tell you a specific type that he wants you to sign? There are some benefits to having a power of attorney. Since power of attorney allows the person you choose to handle your affairs if you cannot do so yourself, you must completely trust the person you're giving this power to. It can also give you peace of mind and reassurance that there is someone you chose who would have the authority to act for you in the event of an emergency or if you became incapacitated.

Power of attorney can differ, depending on when you want the power to begin and end, or how much responsibility you want to give that person, also known as the Agent. There is a Conventional power of attorney. This one begins when you sign it and continues until you become mentally incapacitated. There is the Durable power of attorney that also begins when you sign it and stays in effect for your lifetime. Then there is the Springing power of attorney. This one begins only when a specific event happens, such as when you become incapacitated or mentally unable.

I don't know exactly how busy you are, but really think about power of attorney. Remember, you must really trust the person you are giving this power to. You have only known him for five months. Do you think that is enough time to really trust someone? I cannot speak for you, but if it were me, I would not give him power of attorney at this point. Seriously look into the pros and cons of giving power of attorney to anyone.

Situation

16 High Gas, Low Cash

If the price of fuel doesn't go down, I'll have to ride the bus everywhere I need to go. I live in a place where everyone drives. You can't get many places if you don't. I have a Honda and I get good fuel mileage, but even so I still need to find ways to complete my chores without consuming so much fuel. I spend about $47 per week on fuel. At the end of the week, I don't know where it all went. And I hadn't even completed all of my errands.

Can you suggest ways to preserve fuel?

Response

This is a common concern for so many people. There are ways you can save on fuel. If you keep regular maintenance, your car will run more efficiently and burn less fuel. You will need to have regular oil changes, air filter replacements and properly inflated tires. Drive smart and not aggressively. Aggressive driving leads to increased acceleration and braking that can use unnecessary fuel. Try to maintain a steady speed for as long as possible and use the cruise control over long distances. Change your daily commute. If you commute through heavy, stop-and-go, rush hour traffic, you might consider driving to and from work an hour earlier or later in order to miss the rush. Avoiding that kind of traffic cannot only save on fuel, but also create a less stressful drive.

Another good way to save fuel is to combine errands. Plan your travel in order to maximize your time on the road. If you can, plan trips to the grocery store, dry cleaners, or any other errands so they are all part of your daily commute. There is no need to make a separate trip if you pass these locations on a daily basis. Last but not least, you may even consider a hybrid. Purchasing a new vehicle may be costly up front, but the savings in gasoline usage can pay for itself. Combine this with a potential tax credit for purchasing a hybrid and you may be able to save hundreds of dollars a year.

Situation

17 I Need Some Help
(Payday Loans)

I need a little help to bridge me over until my first disability check kicks in. I work for the Post Office as a mail carrier. I slipped and fell, and broke my arm. I was trying to get away from a dog and made a bad step, landing on my arm. The disability insurance office told me that I would start getting a check in the mail last week, but it has not come yet. I've been out of work for a few weeks now, but I really need some money to hold me over.

My roommate said, "Don't worry, girl. I will take care of things until you get some money coming in."

Now my car note is due, and I really don't expect her to pay that for me, too. In fact, I know she would not be able to do that. I went on the Internet and found a payday loan company. I filled out the application and got approved for $500.00. If I agree to this, they could have the money in my account by tomorrow morning.

A friend of mine told me about this. It worked for her, but just for a while. She got into big trouble because she took out a $1,000 loan and couldn't pay the whole amount back in the two weeks they give you. She ended up having to pay $300 every two weeks. In all, she paid $1500 back in just interest and still had to pay another $1500. This turned out to be a nightmare for her. She lost more than it was worth. She had to pay $3,000.00 in ten weeks.

I know I have to pay back the $500, with interest in two weeks. I believe I can do this if my check comes in on time. This is just a chance I have to take because I am behind on my car note. Do you think this is something I should do?

Response

I will say this about payday loans: they really look attractive to many people because the money is available overnight. If you can help it, my advice is to steer clear of payday loans. It does seem like you need it. Since you know that there is some money coming in, it might be a better financial move for you to call the company that financed your car and possibly, you can make arrangements to pay them later. The price of paying them later might not cost you as much as the interest on your payday loan. This is just a suggestion, but worth the try.

In the event that you must take the payday loan, my advice is to not take more than 10% of your actual paycheck or in your case, your disability check. That way, paying the loan will be much easier to do. My wish for you is that your disability check comes on time, or at least when you are expecting it so that you can take care of your business and put your focus on getting that arm healed. You can then return to work and all of this will be over for you.

Situation

18 Who's Looking At You?
(Inquiries on Your Credit Report)

Last Saturday Night my three girlfriends and I went to the concert by the sea. It is a big summer jam and we go every year. Every year one of us is the designated driver and this year was my turn.

My car is much too small for all of us, so I called a car rental place a couple of days early to ensure that on the day I needed the car it would be available. The car that I chose was the black-on-black Escalade. The day of the concert I went to the car rental place a few of hours early so I would have time to get the car, pick up my girls, and party a little before the concert started. When I got to the car rental place, the agent had the Escalade ready. After I presented my debit card and driver's license, the agent told me he had to pull my credit report. It disturbed me, but what could I do if I wanted the car. I had never heard of a car rental place pulling your credit report to rent a car. He said it's done all the time.

After the brief delay, I got the Escalade. All went well. I picked up my girls and made the concert with 15 minutes to spare. My girls and I had a great night out and the Escalade was a perfect choice. I want to know can anyone just pull your credit report the way the agent did at the car rental place.

Response

I am so glad you asked this question because the answer is "no." No one is allowed to pull your credit report unless you give him or her authorization to do so. The Fair Credit Reporting Act spells out exactly who can pull your credit and why. It is called Permissible Purpose. Here are the guidelines that define Permissible Purpose.

1. At your request. We all have the right to access and view our own individual credit report.

2. In response to a court order or subpoena. This typically happens in credit related lawsuits involving lenders, consumers, and/or credit reporting agencies.

3. In relation to a credit application. When you apply for a loan, the lender is granted permission to pull your credit report to determine your eligibility. Your existing lenders also are legally allowed to periodically pull your credit report for account review purposes.

4. For pre-employment screening. Your potential employer has the right to pull your credit reports when determining employment eligibility.

5. For purposes of insurance underwriting. Even

though most people disagree with this one, insurance companies are legally allowed to use your credit reports to determine your insurance premiums, and whether or not they want to issue you a policy at all.

6. In an attempt to collect a debt. If you default on a loan or owe an unpaid debt, lenders and/or debt collection agencies have the right to pull your credit report for the purpose of collecting a debt.

7. In relation to child support. Credit reports can be assessed to determine an individual's capacity or ability to pay child support.

If you inquire into who's accessing your credit report and find someone who is not on the list I just gave you, report that activity to the police. It should be reported in case there is identity theft involved. But in your case I can see why you allowed him to pull your report. You needed to rent the car. Although you may not have liked it, many companies that never pulled credit in the past are now doing so.

The best advice I can give you is to use a credit card to rent a car. Most car rental agencies will not pull your credit if you use a credit card rather than the debit card. You can also call them beforehand and ask if they pull credit reports. If they do, find one that does not.

I am glad the night went well for you and your girls.

Situation

19 The Cost Of Prison

My husband was recently convicted of a crime and is going to be in prison for the next two years. He has been in the local jail for the last seven months, and the financial burden of him being there is taking its toll. When I say financial burden, I do not mean the burden of paying a lawyer and losing his income, but the hardship of communication alone. It was very difficult for him to cope with being away from us and locked up so he called at least twice a day to talk to the children and me during his first few months in jail. Since direct calling is not allowed, he had no choice but to call collect. When we got the first bill for the collect calls, it was over $800, and this was only one month's worth of calls! I could not believe it. Fortunately, my income was enough to pay the bill and keep the lines of communication open.

I really want to be there for my husband. I don't want him to be out of touch with our kids. Since he has been sentenced to prison for such a long time, I know that we will not be able to afford $800 phone bills every month. However, it's very difficult for me to tell him that he can't call home as often as he'd like. I feel absolutely awful about this, but something must be done. I need someone to give me some ideas or suggestions on how to deal with this?

Response

I am so sorry that you and your family are dealing with this kind of situation. Unfortunately, the jails are full of fathers and husbands, and it creates a serious burden on the spouses and family members who choose to support them. I know someone who went through a similar experience with her fiancé.

Maybe I can give you some advice based on what she told me. The first thing you have to do is decide to create a budget that will allow your husband to communicate with his family, but also be strong enough to enforce that budget. It was very difficult for this woman's fiancé to deal with being in prison, locked away like he was. That is why he called her non-stop. Obviously, your husband is having a similar hard time. But if you don't enforce the budget, it will become more difficult for him. Additionally, the phone bill will become so high that you may not be able to pay it. Then what will he do when he can't reach you and the kids at all?

The emotional turmoil that you and your husband are going through is impossible to imagine. But you have to be the one to take the stand and help him understand that not communicating as much by phone is the only way to make sure you can communicate at all. I suggest that you take the time to help communicate with your husband by writing letters as much as you possibly can and have him to do the same. You can write him four days out of the week, and alternately talk four days out of the next week. Also, have each of the children write letters to him.

This will take effort on all parties, but in the long run, you may end up saving thousands of dollars on phone calls. Think about what you both can do with a nest egg like that. It can help him start a business, something that will help him get back on his feet. It is very hard to be in your position, but I encourage you to stay strong and make those decisions that will benefit all of you in the long run.

Situation

20 Who Needs Online Banking

I am set in my ways. I've been like this for a long time. My son has said I need to do my banking online. I'm not about to do that. All I'm going to do online is get information. And that's that. I told my son and daughter in-law they are just tired of taking me to the bank every Wednesday. That's really what I think it is. I have other people that can take me if they don't want to. My friend down the street will take me. I have even told my son that. My son tells me not to ask my neighbor; he doesn't mind taking me.

If he doesn't have a problem with it, why is he always telling me to do my banking online? I don't trust putting all my pertinent information on the Internet. One of those hackers could get in there, steal my information and take all of my money. So why is that boy of mine pushing me to do that? I think it's his wife! Well, he better get used to it. He can talk 'til he's blue in the face. I am not budging. The only banking I'm doing at home is balancing my checkbook.

Do you think I'm right?

Response

I really understand your concern about online banking. Many people who are set in their ways are uncomfortable with change. Just to ease your mind, it does work. There was a recent study done about online banking, and the incident of fraud was less than one percent over the course of the last five years.

I don't know why your son is so persistent, but I'm sure it's nothing more than his desire for you to keep up with the times. He knows how convenient it is for those that do their banking online. Bankers actually encourage online banking because it saves them time and money on the mailing. Every day billions of dollars are transacted through online banking. Checking your balances, reviewing your accounts are all made easier and faster online.

The next time you are in the bank, ask your banker about the security features used to keep your information safe if you were to bank online. Maybe by knowing more about how it works, you will decide that online banking is for you. If not, then continue to transact your financial business in a way that satisfies you.

Situation

21 Piggybacking
(Is It For Me?)

Someone once told me about a credit improvement process called piggybacking. This was a while ago when I was looking into buying a home. According to this person, piggybacking would help improve my credit scores which were not high. I didn't have a lot of negative information on my report, but I did not have a lot of good information, either.

I had decided to wait and work on improving my credit scores instead of getting into something I did not understand. Piggybacking is still a mystery to me.

Can you please explain just what is piggybacking? Is it legal?

Response

It is a good thing that you decided to take the time to build up your credit scores instead of jumping into something you really did not know anything about.

Piggybacking is not illegal, but it does involve another person's credit. This is how it works. The process of piggybacking is when someone adds another person to his or her credit account in order to help that person develop a positive credit profile. The credit will then be attributed to both parties. This is something many parents do for their children when they turn 18 years old in order to help them.

The result of piggybacking is a credit profile that does not represent an accurate picture to someone who is considering providing you with credit. That is why most companies are trying to eliminate these types of piggyback accounts through the credit bureau.

So, if you don't want to go through all of these extras, then waiting to build a solid good credit score is a wise thing to do.

Situation

22 How Did My Gift Card Get Scammed?

I wanted to get a gift for my friend who was graduating from nursing school. I originally intended to buy her a few painting canvases. I knew she would appreciate that because she paints in oils. It's her hobby, and she paints beautifully! But this day, I was running late.

I couldn't miss her graduation, but I hadn't gotten the canvases as I had hoped. In order to get something to recognize her achievement, I stopped at Wal-Mart and purchased a $100 gift card. I gave it to her right after the graduation party. A few days later, she called to tell me that the gift card I had given her only had a few dollars on it.

This was very strange to me because I went online the day after I purchased the card to ensure that it had been activated and it was. The $100 I had placed on the card was there. I was puzzled so I called Wal-Mart's Customer Service and told them about the discrepancy. Even though I was not able to prove that I was not the one who used the card, they were nice enough to send me a replacement card.

While I am appreciative of having received a

replacement, I would still like to know how someone was able to use the gift card that had been in my friend's possession the entire time.

Response

You probably wish you had more time that day to go to the art store and buy your friend the canvases you really wanted her to have. You would have saved so much time not having to deal with the gift card nightmare. It would seem that the only explanation for the card being used is that someone took it from your friend's possession, used it, repackaged it and then returned it, without her ever noticing. Not likely.

Fortunately, there is a much simpler explanation for this, and it is happening all over the country with gift cards from many retail stores like Wal-Mart, Home Deport, Best Buy, and many others. This is a scam that has been going on for quite some time. Criminals will go into a store, use their cell phone to take pictures of the account numbers that are on the gift cards at the front of the display rack. Once they have the numbers, they will continue to log onto the store's website to see whether or not it has been activated. If there are available funds on the card that means that an unsuspecting customer came along and actually purchased that gift card. If the account has been activated, the criminal will use the card to make online purchases.

That is how the gift card you purchased was actually used without ever leaving your friend's possession. The best way to protect against this is to purchase a gift card from the back of the rack or request to purchase one that is not on display. If the criminals are never able to get the account number, they will not be able to successfully pull off this kind of scheme.

Situation

23 Teaching My Children About Money

I am a mother of three children. My oldest daughter will turn 13 in a few weeks, and my two sons are nine and seven. As young boys, they always need money for their Xbox 360 game. My husband is doing fine as an attorney, I am doing well in my business, and the children are in good schools. All is well. My concern is balancing between what to give and not give the children.

We want them to have the things they want, but we want them to also understand money. We want them to respect what we do for them and never take it for granted. My daughter has a job on Saturday mornings from 10 to 11AM, with my seven-year-old son teaching him English and reading. An hour later, from 12 to 1PM, she works with my other son, instructing him in math. She wants to earn money to fund her shopping trips to the mall with her friends or go see a movie on Sundays after church.

I came up with this idea so that she can earn money while helping her brothers. It's been working out great. She makes $10 an hour. She thought that was terrific! So now, she makes $20 a week, and the boys are doing well in school.

I want her to understand that she doesn't have to spend every penny she earns just because she has it. How should I start with her?

Response

It is wonderful that you are teaching your children about money early. There are many parents in your position who want their children to be successful, especially when it comes to handling and understanding money. I must say that I really like that idea of having your older daughter tutoring the younger sons and getting paid for it. That's great.

Here are a few simple principles you can use to advance her education about money. Tell your daughter you want her to have her own bank account. She will be very excited about that, I'm sure. Go to the bank and open a custodial bank account in her name. This type of an account will allow you to make deposits and manage the account with her. Let her make the opening deposit and order the checks on her own. When she gets her checkbook, teach her how to write checks to pay bills. She will love the responsibility of doing this! It will make her feel like she is growing up, because at 13, she is. Sit down with her and teach her how to create a budget. The budget needs to include items she wants to buy, others she wants to do for fun and basic responsibilities, such as saving some of her money for the future.

It is up to parents to teach children early about money and how to handle and manage it. If they understand how it all works, they will become more aware of having and using money in the best way. This is also a great introduction for them toward a healthy and successful attitude about their finances as an adult.

Situation

24 Where Is All My Money Going?

(Taxes)

My wife and I are both executives in a Fortune 1,000 marketing company. We both make over $100-thousand a year, and we live a very comfortable lifestyle. For the most part, we are very happy with where we are in our lives now. We have put some money away for our retirement, but as we get older, we are starting to wonder whether we have put away enough.

Each year when we look at what we make and what we spend, we find that a significant portion of our out-going money is in taxes. We certainly have no problems paying taxes, but we are seriously looking for ways to reduce the amount of tax burden we have each year. Do you know of any specific plan or formula that we can use to help us minimize our taxes each year?

Response

Living in America is wonderful, and the American system is one that works because of the tax dollars that we all pay. Taxes support the country, but that does not mean anyone wants to pay more taxes than he absolutely has to. I have talked to so many people that are looking for ways to reduce taxes, and what I have found is that reducing your taxes is about understanding the basics and having a good plan.

The three basic ways to reduce your taxes are by reducing your income, increasing your deductions, and taking advantage of tax credits. When you and your wife are working on a plan to reduce your taxes, the reduction of income is the most important. It just makes sense that the less money you make, the less taxes you will pay. Overall, the best way to reduce your income is to contribute money to a 401k, or some other type of retirement plan at work. Your contribution will help your wages, which will lower your taxes. You can also lower your income through adjustments to the income. This can be under adjusted gross income such as contributions to an IRA, moving expenses, although you may never need this one, the payment of alimony and the payment of interest on student loan and classroom or education related expenses.

The second formula for decreasing your taxes is to increase your tax deductions. Three of the biggest tax deductions that you can take are the payments of interest on your mortgage, the payment of state taxes and gifts to charities, and finally, take advantage of tax credits for college expenses. There is a tax credit called the lifetime learning credit, and it is for anyone taking college classes, no matter the age or the discipline studied.

Reducing the amount of taxes you pay each year does take some work, some research and some creativity. But it can be done. I would highly recommend that you seek the counsel of a qualified financial advisor before making any final decisions.

Situation

25 Gold Digging, Who Me?

I really don't think I am a gold-digger, but my friends would say different. Men are very attracted to me not because I am so beautiful, but because I am self-assured, confident, and have a positive attitude. I show appreciation when they speak to me.

Some of my girlfriends are just the opposite: some are more attractive, some standoffish, and some even play hard to get. In the end, men are attracted to me because I am attracted to them. I must add however, that I am only attracted to men with money. After all, what can a guy who has no money do for you?

When my girlfriends ask me about love, my responses are either, "what about it?" or "what about the money?"

I can't see their point of view when they are doing the same things I am. And they're not even guaranteed love!

So I say, "No money, no honey!"

You see, this is what I believe: if you hang around a man long enough, you could fall in love with him. I make sure that doesn't happen to me. I avoid the risk of falling in love with a poor man by never hanging around them.

The bottom line is that I think my friends are jealous of me because of the fabulous trips I take all over the world. The closest they get to those places is the postcard I send them. I wear designer clothes, handbags, and shoes. Diamonds are truly my best friends. One thing, however, that my friends don't know about me is that my men, and there are a few, deposit money in my personal account every week.

I don't understand why they think I'm a gold-digger. I am just smarter than they are. What fool would want to be in love with a poor man? He can't take you anywhere. He can't supply you with little things. He can't even help you in the case of an emergency. Besides, I hate jealousy. It seems to me that poor men are a more jealous type. If a wealthy man sees someone trying to get your attention, he is just going to do more for you. At least that is my experience.

Can you tell me what is wrong with these so-called friends of mine?

Response

I cannot tell you about your friends or who your friends really are. I can tell you about the financial aspect of what you have told me about your relationships. It seems as though your relationships are more like business transactions, and the men you involve yourself with are merely business partners. If this is the way you are living your life, I am sure you have your reasons.

I have some concerns because I never heard you say a word about your future. There are so many young, beautiful people who live for right now - never thinking about old age or a pension plan of some sort. I am sure you will be attractive at any age, but what do you have to offer other than the obvious? Think about it. What happens to you when a boyfriend starts spending on younger women who are doing the same thing you are? It gets old real fast! If you are saving money or putting money away for the future, I will say you are at least thinking beyond the right now.

I do want to say one thing about your point of view on poor men versus rich men. I do not believe because a man is poor that he is more jealous than a man who is wealthy. Most jealously comes from a place of insecurity. Every man who is not wealthy is not insecure and conversely, every wealthy man is not secure. I am sure there are many who would disagree with your philosophy of life. I would like to see all women be smart about their future, by saving and investing for tomorrow.

Situation

26 IRS

(Red Flags)

I used to be a sales representative for a produce company owned by two men. It was a very successful business. In the five years I was with the company, I learned everything about the produce business. I knew all of the companies to buy from and all of the companies to sell to. They all liked me, particularly the way I conducted business. I felt certain that I could duplicate that I learned and achieve the same success.

When I told them that I was going out on my own, I got all the help I needed. Now my company is three years old and growing. I hired a CPA who does a great job, but I always want to make sure that I am doing all I can to save in the right places and not spend wastefully. I have never been audited, and I never want to be.

What should or shouldn't I do to make sure that my company is never audited?

Response

Your concerns are legitimate. No one wants to get a visit from the IRS. It is good that you have a CPA that does a great job for you, especially someone you trust.

I am not a CPA, but I will tell you that a friend of mine gave me some good pointers on how best to avoid an IRS audit. He called them the "red flags." One of the red flags is to make sure you are not overpaying a child or close relative that works in your business. Another red flag is to report an excessively high income compared to previous years. It is possible to have a high income one year, and while there is nothing wrong with that, be aware that it could increase the possibility of an audit. You also want to make sure that your federal tax return is proportionate with your state tax return. Inconsistency between federal and state tax returns is a sure way to trigger an IRS audit.

The IRS is very good at detecting activities that could be considered illegal. Make sure that you trust and/or are comfortable with the person who prepares your taxes. In any event, if you ever are selected for an audit, make sure you protect yourself by retaining knowledgeable representation. You do not want to stand before the IRS without any assistance. Make sure you keep your paperwork in order and are able to answer any questions that could be asked.

Continued success in your produce business.

Situation

27 My Mother Wants A Reverse Mortgage

My Mother turned 64 a few months ago. Ever since she was 62, she has been talking about this reverse mortgage thing. Mom has two children, my brother who is 41, and myself. I am 38. As the daughter, I have always been there to sort of take care of her since my father's death 15 years ago.

Mom has slowed down and her health is declining. I have talked to her about doing this reverse mortgage. I told her that we would look into it and make a decision after learning about the pros and cons. She said okay, and I never heard her speak about it again until now. I want to really know how it works, and I don't want her to go to a bank or a company and do this until I look into it.

My first concern is who will get her home when she passes. My brother and I have our own homes, and we are doing well. But we don't want someone to take her home because she did not understand everything she signed. I just want my Mom to live her life happily and enjoy it because she deserves it. Still, there are so many questions to be answered first. What do you think about reverse mortgages?

Response

Your mother is a very lucky lady to have a daughter who is looking after her concerns. You are absolutely right to get all of the information you can about reverse mortgages. Since this is a financial arrangement concerning the elderly, it is prudent that your family members research and be there for them.

There are many elderly people getting scammed and taken advantage of when they don't have someone looking out for them. There are a few basic facts about reverse mortgages you need to know first. A reverse mortgage is a loan against your home. But this loan works the opposite way: instead of you paying the bank, the bank pays you. It could be a fixed stream of money until you or the last surviving borrower dies or sells the home. It could be up-front money or regular monthly payments. This loan does not need to be paid on as long as you live in the house. Over time, the more money to bank lends you, the larger your debt. With each payment you collect from the bank, the equity in your home is reduced. It will be up to the lender to tell you how big of a loan you qualify for, based on your age and home value.

The pros are: you can't lose your home, you keep

the title and ownership of your house, and to get this loan, credit, income or employment is not a consideration. The cons include you will not be able to leave the home free and clear for your children because the loan is paid back after the borrower's death. By selling the property, it will be the total of the payment received plus interest.

These are the facts about reverse mortgages. A few places to look to learn more about them include the AARP publication, Home Made Money, a consumer's guide to reverse mortgage, which is also available on the website www.aarp.com and the National Reverse Mortgage Lenders Association. It is very important to understand as much as you can about these loans, and I am sure that you will.

Good luck to you and your Mom. If she does decide to do this, I hope she can enjoy the decision and her life to the fullest.

Situation

28 I'm Scared To Ask For Money

I am a college graduate, with an engineering degree. I have always wanted to be in business for myself, but life had to play out first. I married a fantastic woman, and we have three children. My wife and I are both in our mid 40s, and our children are grown.

I have recently been laid off from my job because of cutbacks. For the most part, I worked consistently up until last year. Due to the layoff and the fact that my wife only works part-time because of her health, my bills fell behind. My credit scores are now low as a result of these unfortunate events.

Nevertheless, I am in the process of launching a new business venture. I will need in excess of a hundred thousand dollars in order to effectively launch this venture. This has been something I've worked on for a number of years, and now is the time to make it happen. My problem is that I cannot get a loan of that size from a bank because of my low credit score, and I do not have enough collateral to back it up.

My only option is to go to private investors. I have

some relationships with people that could invest in my venture, but I find it very difficult to ask for money. I am between a rock and a hard place on this one. Is this a common feeling for anyone who has to ask for money for a business?

Response

It all depends on how you look at it. This is a very common problem among small business owners. Fortunately, there is a very simple solution to your problem. Being afraid is the number one reason why so many people never achieve their goals. They are afraid for some reason or another. For some, it may be insecurity; for others, it may be pride, but I always say this - DON'T LET FEAR STOP YOU FROM WALKING INTO YOUR DESTINY. When you ask for money for your business, that is just what it is - a business deal. Business people understand that. It will not look like you are needy because you are asking for money for your business. That should make you feel a lot better about asking.

Look at effective fund raising from private investors like a partnership - you come together to make both parties win. You always want to show your investors that it is a WIN-WIN situation. If they invest in your venture or company, they too, will win from the merger. This is one of the surest reasons you will hear that big word YES.

To be a business owner or to launch a vision you have for your venture, you must truly believe in what you are doing. If you do believe, then you will be driven by the passion it will bring. Owners and leaders must be tough enough to make good business decisions. That means you cannot be afraid. Remember - don't let fear stop you from following your dream.

So step out of your fear and go make your list of everyone you can think of with the money you need. Call them, tell them what you need, and ask for it. Show them how you both can win. Look at the bright side - they may need exactly what you are bringing to them. That is called a WIN-WIN situation!

Situation

29 My Ungrateful Sister

(It's Not On My Credit Report)

I am the kind of person who takes pride in paying my bills on time. I had a perfect record with my phone company, until I did my younger sister a favor: I got her a phone and put it on my plan. I did this for her because she was coming to my state to go to college.

I did not realize how much my parents spoiled her. I am the oldest, so I was gone and on my own when I was 20 years old. My little sister was only ten when I left home, but boy, they certainly raised her differently than how they raised me. I was very responsible at her age. My sister, on the other hand, has a very irresponsible attitude and because of this, having her on my account ruined my good standing with my phone company. Lil' Sis ran my phone bill sky high.

I didn't realize she was not paying her part of the phone bill until my phone was turned off. I had to pay a very large sum of money in order to have it turned back on. In the meantime, it took me almost a year to pay off the bill she created. I did get another phone, but my boyfriend got the phone under his plan for me. Wow! Never again will I do a favor for a relative.

Recently, I looked at my credit report, and all the years of paying on time were never recorded. I was shocked! Can you please tell me why my payment history from those creditors I paid on time does not appear on my credit report?

Response

How unfair! Your little sister does not realize how good she has it - to have an older sister in the town where she attends college and to have someone who is there for her. So many young people starting out have to do it all alone. Somewhat the way you had to.

I do understand what Lil' Sis did has made you realize how times have changed, even in parenting. Maybe, because your parents went through everything with you, by the time Lil' Sis came along they just weren't the same as they were ten years before.

Now let's talk about your phone bill. Your cell phone carrier decided not to report your account. There are many companies that do not report accounts, such as your water bill, your light bill, and your phone bill. Now, I am not saying you don't need to pay these bills on time because I assure you that if you don't, that negative history will be reported to your credit.

I definitely agree it seems unfair that your negative

history will be reported, while your positive history is not. It is certainly unfair that there are many bills you have paid and continue to pay on time that will not be reported to credit bureaus. Unfortunately, that is the way it is.

Maybe if enough people complain about this to the companies, something could change and compel them to report positive payment history, as well. Maybe as your sister grows up and sees the real world, she will respect the gifts and privileges you provided for her.

In any case, continue to be the person that you are, that is, a positive role model for your Little Sister.

Situation

30 A Hole In My Sandbag!

(Paying Interest)

I have noticed on my credit card statements I am paying almost 17 percent interest on all of my transactions. It has me wondering why I am paying so much and why don't I have any control over it?

My credit cards are sinking me! Every month I only pay the interest, which averages a few hundred dollars. Now after I pay all of that money for the interest, I still cannot use my card because I have not paid any money on the principal. I really feel upset that I can't use my card, especially since I am out $200 to $300 per month.

I told my husband it feels like there is a hole in my sandbag. My money is leaking out of my pockets, and I have nothing to show for it. I am trying very hard to stay on top of my bills so that my credit can stay in good standing, but this just does not feel right. Please explain this interest thing to me.

Response

I understand why you would say there is a hole in your

sandbag because there is. You see, when it comes to interest, the credit card companies have the authority to adjust your interest at will. The reason you don't have control over the rates is because the banks set them based on certain factors:

- Your personal credit score
- Your length of credit history
- Your income
- Your overall risk potential

The window of hope rests in some recent legislation that promises to be helpful in this regard.

The control you do have over interest rates is to not get caught in the credit card game. Stay away from them. If you do have credit cards, do not spend more than what you can afford to pay at the end of the month. Look at interest rates as if they are the cost of the money. If you carry a balance on your credit cards, always pay more than the minimum amount. If you are only paying the minimum payment on your credit card, you are barely paying interest, which means it may take years to pay off even the smallest balance.

Just remember this important fact when you are dealing with credit cards, if you are going to use them, be sure to pay them off at the end of the month. That will help you avoid the hole in your sandbag trap, and you will benefit from using the credit cards instead of the credit cards benefiting from you.

Situation

31 I Can't Believe What I Heard

(Foreclosing On My Home)

This is the craziest thing I have ever heard and a real nightmare that I actually lived. This is my story. I purchased my home eight years ago when I was a single woman. When I made the purchase, I had been working for many years. My credit was great, and my bills were always paid on time. Three years ago, I met my husband. We got married two years ago when he was just starting a new job. Everything was going well. I knew he didn't have much when we met, so he moved into my house. And then, I suddenly loss my job! I didn't panic because I had a substantial nest egg, so I continued to pay my bills as usual.

Six months into the marriage, I found out I was pregnant, so I asked my husband to pay the mortgage because I was not working, pregnant, and my savings was getting very low. He was making a very good salary on his job, but I could not believe what I heard.

He said to me, "If you want me to pay the mortgage, you will have to sign your home over to me. Put the home in my name, and my name only."

I thought he was kidding. He made it clear he was

not.

We live in a community property state. Since I owned our home before our marriage, if we divorced, he could not touch my house. I did not sign the home over to him. Why would he want me to do that before he would pay a dime on the mortgage? He was living there, also. I continued to pay for as long as I could.

When our baby was born, there was tension in our marriage. He took care of everything in the house and the baby's expenses when I ran out of money, but would not pay a dime on the house. The house may go into foreclosure. We are now separated, and I am losing my house. Is there anything I can do to save it?

Response

Wow! What a selfish thing for your husband to do. It is obvious he went into the marriage for the wrong reason. I am sorry this happened to you. I can imagine the hurt and devastation you must have gone through.

The first thing is to start communicating with your mortgage company. If not, it is only going to make a bad situation worse. If there is any possibility of keeping your home out of foreclosure, your mortgage company will most likely work with you to reach that solution. They could work out something until you secure another job. One of the options possibly available to you is to work out an extension on your mortgage where they extend the grace period on late payments up to six months. This does not happen often, but in your situation, it would be justifiable to request it.

If you are finding that you are not getting any cooperation from the bank on an extension, you may want to negotiate a restructuring of your mortgage. If you do reach some type of agreement with the bank, make sure that you get that agreement in writing. The reason you want it in writing is because it will help you when negotiating with other creditors. If they see that your mortgage company is willing to work with you, then they will also be more likely to extend you some consideration. If none of these things prove successful, you will want to consider a difficult option of selling your home. In these times, there is really no solution that is a comfortable one.

The worst case is to lose your home to foreclosure. At least, if you sell your home you will be in the potential position of having some money left over to work on securing a new place to live. Being in the position of losing your home can be a nightmare. When you are going through this situation, you want to do your best to make calm and rational decisions. A bad decision will make this situation much worse. Right now is the time to be focused on doing what is best for your son and you. Anything that is lost can be recovered. But you have to be willing to make those difficult decisions.

I do wish you the best during this difficult time and hope you are able to come to a successful resolution with your mortgage company. This will also give you time to decide what to do about your marriage. I really hope you make the right decision here, also. A man like that does not seem to care about anyone but himself.

Situation

32 My Perfect Little Home
(The Adjustable Rate Mortgage)

My husband and I want to buy a new house. We saw a very small, two-bedroom home that fits our present needs. Since we are just starting out, I believe that a cozy, intimate home, with a lovely front yard and nice size backyard suits us perfectly. I suggested to my husband that we stay in the home for about three years, for it would be a nice starting point from which we can build. Then, we can sell the place and move into a larger, four-bedroom home. That is when I'd like to start our family. My husband is in agreement with me.

Our mortgage broker suggested that we could purchase under an Adjustable Rate Mortgage. I have heard some uncomplimentary things about this type of mortgage. With adjustable rate mortgages, your payment could possibly increase over the life of the mortgage. If this is the case, can you explain why we should consider it?

Response

As a new homebuyer, the benefits of buying a home

under an adjustable rate mortgage are in your favor - if you do not plan to stay in the home for a long time. That kind of mortgage is advantageous if you are buying this home as your first home with plans of upgrading to a larger home within the next three to five years, which seems to be the case for your husband and you. Another reason the adjustable rate mortgage is beneficial to you is because you are getting into the home with a low monthly payment. By the time the rate increases, you will be ready to sell, lease it to someone else, or refinance at a lower fixed rate.

While adjustable rate mortgages have their benefits, many people have gotten into serious financial trouble with them because the monthly payment could almost double at the time of the adjustment. If you are a person with credit problems, you may want to seriously consider a fixed rate mortgage instead of an adjustable rate mortgage. The main reason is that if your rate is about to go up and you are unable to refinance, you could find yourself facing a potential foreclosure because you cannot afford the new rate.

Buying a home is always a process that should be taken very seriously. All factors should be considered. Fixed rate mortgages have advantages and disadvantages, just like adjustable rate mortgages. Please make sure that you and your husband take the time to do the research to ensure that you are making the best possible decision.

Enjoy your new home, it sounds like a lovely place!

Situation

33 Security For A Six Year Old

(Life Insurance)

My husband and I have two children, ages six and four. We have been very disciplined in saving and buying bonds for our children's futures. My major concern, however, is life insurance. When I was nine years old, my father died. One minute he was there; the next, he was gone. It left my mother devastated. She only had a job babysitting the neighbors' children, so when Dad died, life changed forever. There was no insurance, no savings - nothing. My two older brothers had to get jobs after school to help make ends meet. They were 14 and 12 years old. We really struggled my whole childhood.

I have life insurance from my job now, and my husband does, as well. I feel it isn't enough. My husband thinks we are covered, that we have nothing to worry about, and that we should just relax. He believes that I have this built in fear because of what happened to my family when my father died, and maybe, I do.

Do you think this is something I should be so concerned about?

Response

Yes! Yes! Yes! I do think you should be as concerned as you are. What happened to you as a child was very traumatic, I'm sure. Losing a parent so suddenly is hard for any child. Because you went through rough times as a child, it made a certain mark on you forever. I really can see why you feel the insurance your husband and you have is not enough. Even though the insurance you have at work may cost only a few dollars a month, you still may want to look into more insurance.

I think you are absolutely correct. It would be best if you and your husband get your own insurance, independent of your jobs. Because if you ever get laid off, fired, or must leave the job for any reason, will the job give you the life insurance? Most likely not! That is not good. I would say keep the insurance on the job, but please get another life insurance policy for your family. I would also advise against a cash value policy and go with the level term policy. You get more coverage at a lower cost.

Situation

34 My Boyfriend And The Stock Market

(Learning How It Works)

Recently, I decided to become involved in the stock market. It is something I've always wanted to do. However, I don't know much about how it actually works. I had a boyfriend once who was thoroughly familiar with it. He would talk endlessly about his portfolio, what he traded, what he bought. It was like speaking to me in a foreign language. I tried to ask some questions but it was all above my head. That was many years ago. I couldn't grasp it or maybe he was a bad teacher. I'll never know as he and I broke up a long time ago. Now I am ready to buy some shares of stock. I know that in order to buy them, I need to go through a company like Ameritrade.

Could you please help me understand more about the stock market and how it works?

Response

Understanding the stock market can be very complex. It is based on a company's need to raise money in order to operate. To raise money, a company can do what is called "going public," where it offers to sell shares of stock in that company for a set price. The price of the shares and the number of shares offered are set prior to an initial public offering (IPO). Once these shares are issued, they are then sold and traded on the New York Stock Exchange, Nasdaq, or singular market. These exchanges are where investors buy and sell stock in the company they are interested in. That's where you come in. When you buy shares of stock in a company, it takes shares away from the amount available, which makes the price go up. It is very similar to the concept of supply and demand. When a lot of people are buying stocks in a company, it causes stock prices to go up. When a lot of people are selling, it causes the stock prices to go down. Since you are looking to become involved, you must understand that the stock market is not a place to get rich quick.

You should make sure that you either have qualified advice before buying and/or selling or make sure that you have done your research. There are many places on line that provide the resources you will need to make good decisions when buying stock. Never invest what you cannot afford to lose! There are no guarantees with any type of investment and the stock market is no exception. This can be an exciting venture for you. Make sure it is an enjoyable one by making informed decisions with your money.

Situation

35 Me And My Dad

(Taking Care Of Dad)

I recently brought my father home to stay with me. He is 79 years old, and his health is fair. Dad has Parkinson's and some dementia. I am an only child, so there is no one that can help me. I lost my Mother when I was 14 years old, so it was Dad who raised me. He always said, "Me and my boy. We will make it." Although he took Mom's death very hard, he was strong. The two of us got through. I am divorced and my daughter lives in another state with her three children.

I am really suffering financially, but I don't want to burden my daughter with that. I won't put Dad in a home. It would kill his spirit; even though, he always says, "Son, you can put me in a home. I'll be okay." I know he is saying that because he sees my struggle. It costs a lot of money to hire the nurse that comes to help me two to three days a week. My Dad is really no problem, but he needs constant watch. There is no way I can work my part-time job. Social Security alone is not enough, even with Dad's check. The cost of hiring someone to help me out is more than I can handle. I do need some help because it's all on me.

Response

I certainly can't imagine what you are going through. You have no support with your Dad and your finances are very low, yet, you still must have someone come in to help you. I have found that in your own community, you may find help in your church. Usually, there are members of the church that come in and help the elderly. They can visit a few hours while you run errands or maybe you can make arrangements with a few people to come in and help while you go to work. Some people can cook or bring dinner for your father. Most churches will embrace you and your father. Just get out and ask. I am sure you will find some good people there. Maybe you can do something for the church in return. I'm sure you will find help. That is what churches do; they help people in the community. It may not cost you as much s it does now. Explain your finances to them. Certainly something can be worked out. Keep your spirits up. You are not alone in this. There are many people who would understand and be willing to help you lighten your financial load.

Situation

36 Big Wedding! Big Honeymoon! (No Home)

My husband-to-be wants us to have a big wedding and go on an elaborate cruise for our honeymoon. We have no home. We are living with my older sister right now. We will be moving into a one-bedroom apartment in order to save up enough money to buy a new home in a few years. I don't know what to do at this point. I want a big wedding and a special honeymoon because it is my first time getting married. At the same time, I want to have a home of our own. He keeps telling me that getting married only comes around once in a lifetime and that we can wait to get our home in a few years.

My sister understands my point of view; however, she has suggested that I take the money we plan to spend on the wedding and put it on a down payment for our home. I am so torn. I want us to start our married life together the right way. What would be the best thing for us to do?

Response

Start with this: the best decision will be made when you completely remove emotion and want, and replace them with need. In that case, it would be great to buy your home, plain and simple. But not everything in life is simple, and this situation is certainly not simple.

This is when the two of you really need to sit down and have that conversation, the one that no one likes to talk about - money! If you have not done it before, now is the time. The two of you should talk about your financial values, goals, and habits. This is very important because one of the major problems in relationships is difference in values, goals, and habits. Values are what are important to you and your spouse. Goals are what you want to achieve as a couple, and habits are how you are spending your money and on what.

Gloria Steinem said, “We can tell our values by looking at our checkbook stubs.” Values and habits must come together as one after the marriage. For example, maybe one saves and the other spends. A compromise must be made in such a case. Maybe your habits are not that extreme, but they can be different from one another because differences often come from different upbringing.

If you start with an honest conversation and keep your emotions in check, you will see things a lot clearer and your decisions will be harmonious. If your love is about making each other happy, then my wish for you is to have a happily-ever-after life no matter what you decide to do together.

Situation

37 The 7-Year Pitch

(Items Falling Off Of Your Credit Reports)

I am in the process of cleaning my credit, so I pulled my credit report. I found a few collection accounts on the report that should have fallen off because they are older than seven years. This is not right.

I have always heard that after seven years, certain things fall off the credit report. I see this is not the case. I am very upset because I'm in the process of buying some property, and having this on my credit report can hurt my chances. Why do they give that seven-year pitch if it's not that way at all? What if I didn't check my credit report? I mean, what if I just assumed they did the right thing and dropped the bills after seven years? If I hadn't checked, I would have been stunned to find out when I tried to purchase the property.

I need to have those items off of my credit report. What steps do I take now?

Response

Like you, there are many people who believe as you did - that after seven years, items just go away. Most of them do, but there are a few exceptions.

• Bankruptcies can stay on your report for 10 years.

• A lawsuit or judgment against you can be reported for seven years or until the statute of limitations of the judgment has run out, and most times that is longer than seven years.

• Student loans can be reported for seven years after certain guarantors' actions.

• Tax liens stay on seven years from the date paid.

There are even some collection agencies that update their reporting status to keep the accounts active with the bureaus, which extends the time the account appears on your report.

This is why you must keep records, with dates, even if you are unable to pay at the time. Therefore, if you see this happening on your credit report, you can fight it. If you do challenge it, the bureaus will remove it seven years from origination.

So if you have any of the exceptions on your credit report now, you know why they are there. If none of these aforementioned items appear on your credit report, but there are still items that should be removed, please challenge them. They must be removed. To challenge the items will take a few weeks.

Start now so that you can proceed with your plans. Enjoy your new purchase.

Situation

38 Over The Limit With Being Over The Limit

(Credit Card Companies)

My daughter graduated from college in California, and I wanted to take her to Las Vegas for a mother-daughter celebration trip. I used my credit card that had a $500 credit limit. I am one to watch my credit card spending very carefully. I try to keep the balances on this card low, so that my monthly payment would never be high. This is my "got your back" card. You know, the "in case of something" card.

I used this card for our trip to Las Vegas. I charged $40 for gas because we drove. During our stay, I made sure that I did not spend more than $400 on the card. I paid for everything else with cash. So, that was a total of $440.00. When I recently received my credit card statement, I was quite upset to see a $35.00 over-the-limit fee had been applied. The company charges an annual fee of $65.00, and that charge put my account over my limit of $500. I called and asked why they charged a fee?

I wanted to know if there is anything that can be done to stop the credit card companies from doing this to people.

Response

I'm very sad to say that millions of people had this

same thing happen to them. Credit card companies are allowed to charge an annual fee to your card as long as that fee is disclosed in the card application. When you applied for and signed your name on the application, you agreed to maintain enough available credit on the card to cover the annual fee. Failure to do so results in a forced charge on your card, which in turn means you have to pay a penalty for going over your credit line. While this may seem unfair, it is well within the rights of the credit card company.

The best way to protect yourself is to, first of all, make sure that you always leave enough available credit on the card to cover an annual fee if you know one is going to be assessed within the 30 days of the billing date. The second action you can take is to discontinue using any credit card that charges an annual fee. These are fees not charged by every credit card company. You have to do the research on this. Recently, there has been federal legislation regarding credit card companies' ability to charge these fees. Unfortunately, you will have to pay it.

Always be careful to monitor your credit card spending. Especially note the possibility of any fee taking you over the limit because once you are over the limit, it will cost a lot more to get back under it. I really hope you and your daughter had a great time in Las Vegas. Maybe the next time the two of you go there, you'll have a different card with no annual fee attached.

Situation

39 The Ride Of My Life!

(Buying a New Car)

I am so exited! I am planning to buy my first new car. I have had two pre-owned ones before, but I always managed to buy directly from the owner. So, I have never had the experience of going into a dealership and sitting with the salesman to buy a car. My credit is decent, and I have a few thousand dollars to put down on a new one. Still, I am not sure of what to expect.

I was told that being a young woman going to buy a car alone is not such a good idea. I thought about bringing one of my male friends with me so that I wouldn't look so vulnerable. Do you think that is a good idea? My dream car is the MX-5 Miata. I love that car, and I have been working and saving to buy one for more than a year. I don't want to be too exited in front of the dealer. I want to act like I know what I am talking about, but I am so anxious.

I just don't want to get a bad deal. Other than that, I don't know what to expect or what to ask.

Response

I am excited for you also. It really is a big deal buying a brand new car. It is one of the major purchases in life, so I can see why you feel a bit anxious about the whole thing. Being a young woman and having the discipline to work and save for your car really does say a lot for you in my eyes. You didn't just jump into that car before you were financially ready.

Knowing a former finance manager at a car dealership opened my eyes to many things. I will share them with you so you can have the proper perspective you need to stay on top of the situation. My friend told me they have several tricks in their bag when dealing with an inexperienced buyer. The first trick is to qualify you as a savvy buyer, a sort-of buyer, or a duck. Unfortunately, most first time buyers fall into the latter category. The reason they call them ducks is because they are the ones who are very easy to spot, a very easy target.

When the dealers have a duck on the line, they know it is going to be an easy sale and the buyer will probably fall for any trick in the book. The best way for them to know they have a duck is to ask a simple question: What do you want your payments to be? When you go to buy your car, never answer that question. You will always want to respond to that question by saying, "I want the best deal." This means low interest rate, low down payment, and all of the bells and whistles.

This whole car buying process can be intimidating, and this is why people end up on the short end of the stick. There are more cars, more dealers, and more sellers than there are buyers. With that in mind, you will always have the upper hand. Remember, they need to sell you a car more than you need to buy it from them. This is a long term commitment so you want to make sure you get the best deal for yourself.

Here are some steps I want you to remember:

1. Always ask to meet the finance manager first. This immediately establishes to the sales person that you are there to do business and not play games. When you meet the finance manager, just say hello and something to let them know that you don't have webbed feet. Such as, I just want to meet the person who is going to be responsible for giving me such a great financial deal.

2. When talking about the price of the car, ask to see the dealers invoice. This invoice will show the price the dealer paid for the car. Tell the salesperson you want to start the negotiation at the invoice price and work up from there.

3. Do not take the car until the deal is done. Bailment Agreements that allow you to take the car prior to complete financing are a trap.

4. Never close the deal on the same day. Always take one day to do some research on the offer. You also may want to shop around after you have an approval.

My finance manager friend, who shared these tips, saved me from many disasters. I don't think you need your male friend to go along. I am sure you can handle the car dealer on your own now, so tell your friend to be ready for dinner, and you swing by his house in your brand new shiny MX5-Miata. Your friend will be proud of you. Tell him to hop in and help you celebrate in the new car. Oh, but, please drive safely and sober!

Situation

40 What Alimony? What Child Support?
(This Canít Be For Real)

My husband and I got divorced last year, and it has truly been a strain financially on me. My situation turned out very different than most.

I filed for divorce because of his philandering ways. I really tried to work with him, but I must say my ex is a very sexy man and the women would not leave him alone. I am saying this because I have been present when some women approached him. I can tell you that if I were not there, he would not hesitate to flirt and talk to them. It got to the point where I just couldn't handle it anymore, so I filed for divorce.

He went crazy mad. Not because he didn't want a divorce, but because his ego was bruised. He kept saying, "Who do you think you are, divorcing me?"

Well, he went all out to hurt me and fought for custody of our only daughter. I was working, so he also fought paying alimony because he didn't want to supplement my income. He fought me with lies and deceit. He even slept with the mediator who was supposed to make the final decision on where my daughter was supposed to live. Well, I guess you know how that turned out. The court granted him custody.

He didn't have to pay me any child support, and the alimony was a joke.

I am back in court now to overturn the decision. He has not been happy raising a daughter and neither has my child been happy living with him. She may be six years old, but she knows where she wants to be.

The reason I know how he got custody is because the mediator told me. That's right, she told me herself. How low can a fella go? She told me because she is now feeling used by my ex. He promised her that the two of them would be together, and she believed him. Now that he has what he wanted, which was not to pay me any money, he then dumped her.

It was six months later when she told me about their affair. She claimed she just wanted me to know. She looked at me and said, "Fight to get your child back because he is an awful father."

She also told me that she was out of it from this point; hence, I could not use her in court to testify.

She said, "I just needed you to know the truth."

If I were not so shocked by what she'd just told me, I probably would have punched her in the face.

Awarding him custody while I only get nine days out of a month to see my daughter, has taken a toll on me emotionally, and my credit has suffered, as well. I do have my job, so I am able to stand on my own. Can you tell me where should I even start to build credit again and get myself back on track?

Response

I am sure there is something you can do to find some fair ground here.

First, you will need an attorney who knows child custody law. I would only hope that some parents would see that this selfish, greedy behavior will not only hurt each parent in the long run, but it will forever damage the child. Every child needs its mother, especially if she is a good one. A child needs its father also, but only if the father is looking out for the child and not behaving selfishly as this father is.

I will tell you what steps to take in your situation. Focus on rebuilding your credit first. Open a secured credit card and use it to pay your legal fees. This way you are getting your fees paid as you build your credit. It was this situation that broke your credit down; make it a turn around situation to build your credit back up. Even in the midst of emotional turmoil, one must think logically and use the opportunity for financial growth.

I can only imagine the nightmare you were in before this mediator woman told you the truth. Don't concern yourself with her. Know that if she had the heart to go along with such a wicked plan - that if she doesn't ask God for forgiveness - she will eventually get what's coming to her.

Situation

41 On My New Job

(401k)

After 90 days on the job, I am now a permanent employee and eligible for many company benefits. I have full health insurance, dental, a two-week paid vacation, and five days sick leave.

Next week, I am going to have a meeting with the Human Resources Department because the one benefit I do not really understand is the 401k. I am not clear on how it works and really need to know what it's all about. I know that the 401k is a major benefit a company like this offers, but I don't want to go into the meeting not knowing anything about it.

Response

With a 401k plan, you will have access to a program that allows you to save money now and earn interest on that money, without paying taxes until you reach the age of 65 or over. The tax benefits of contributing to a 401k are substantial. For example, say you invest $4,000 a year into your 401k out of the $60-thousand that is your salary. You would only be taxed on the income - $48,000 - that did not go into the 401k.

A benefit of a 401k plan is that it allows you to create savings for your retirement. Another benefit of the 401k is that your company can match from 25-to-100 percent of your contribution. With a 401k plan, there are a number of ways you can invest for your retirement. These may include mutual funds that invest in the stocks, bond or money markets. Annuities or guaranteed investment pools, company stocks or even self-directed brokerage accounts are also available. Most plans have a selection of investment options that will allow you to create a retirement portfolio. Money can generally be withdrawn from a 401k plan on five different occasions: (1) termination from employment; (2) disability; (3) reaching age 59 1/2 or 55 in some cases; (4) retirement; (5) death.

In the event that you leave the company, you will always be paid the money you put into the 401k and any vested amount due to you from your company's contribution to your account. You will have the option to: (1) keep the account where it is, as long as it is over $1,000; (2) roll it over into a 401k plan at your new company; (3) transfer the money into an IRA at any financial institution; and (4) liquidate your plan to cash. If you liquidate your plan to cash, which is not suggested, you will pay a 10% early withdrawal tax and an additional income tax.

Well, it sounds like you have found a wonderful job. Enjoy your experience on your new job and learn all that you can about your benefits.

Situation

42 I Can't Miss My Soap Operas
(Distractions)

I am almost embarrassed to admit this but I can't miss my soap operas. I am a hairstylist in a very busy beauty salon, so my customers and I are seriously hooked. When it's soap time, all eyes are on the tube and we actually start talking to the characters on the tube like they can hear us. You know, we talk to them just like they are our friend and we know them – putting our two cent in. We have fun.

One day a customer brought her husband to the shop. He sat on the side reading Fortune Magazine.

"DISTRACTED!" the man shouted just as our soap ended.

It echoed throughout the shop. My girls and I looked at each other and then at him.

"Excuse me," one of the ladies said. "What did you say, sir?"

"I bet this goes on in every shop across America," he said.

We all laughed, and he muttered something under his breath.

"Do you have something to say sir?" I asked.

"Yes, ladies, I do."

"The floor is yours." I waved my arms.

And he took it.

"Do any of you ladies know anything about financial empowerment?" he asked

"What are you selling?" I shot back at him.

" Knowledge," he replied with a great deal of confidence in his voice.

"That's enough honey," his wife finally chimed in. "He is a financial advisor, and he doesn't know when he's not at work," she added with pride.

"All I am trying to say," he continued ignoring his wife's admonishment, "is to not be distracted by soaps and TV magazines that get you to pay attention to only what sports figure is sleeping with what woman and what entertainer gets caught stumbling out of what club at three in the morning." He paused as if to let his words soak in. "Distractions, that is what they are. Don't get me wrong, it is perfectly all right to enjoy your shows, but keep it balanced. Read some financial magazines so you can enhance your financial perspectives."

I stopped him right there.

"What a minute," I said. "Do you know I own this shop?"

"Yes," he replied, "but I am talking about owning

more shops. Going bigger. Exercise your financial mind. That is all I am saying. Remember, those who know will always do better and achieve more than those who don't know. Read! If you don't want to read, go to the Wall Street Journal website, or Fortune Magazine website, or any other financial related website, and just expose yourself to it. That's all ladies. I just like to see people know more about the things that matter to one's life and one's lifestyle. That's all."

By this time his wife had paid me, taken his arm and big ole' opinionated mouth right up on out of my shop. I was glad because my next soap opera was just about to come on.

What do you think that was all about?

Response

It's a good thing his wife doesn't get her hair done everyday. It sounds like something is bothering him. Maybe because he is a financial advisor he sees so many people who come to him with little or no knowledge about finances at all, and he thinks that is senseless. Whatever it is, take the good from the bad.

It sounds like he knows his stuff, and maybe he is right! It really could be that many of us are distracted by so many things on the radio or the news that we really don't pay enough attention to the financial world around us or even our own financial world. Maybe if we did, we would be awakened to a whole new world. One day, just check out those websites. You never know what you will find. Look at it this way. At least, you can learn without hearing his big mouth.

Situation

43 Wills Now Or Arguments Later

(The Making of Your Will)

I am a single woman, with a few possessions. Although I am by no means old, I am mid-age. When I turned 50 a few months ago, it hit me, what if something happens to me? What if I die? What will happen to my things? I have worked hard all of my life, and I have acquired some possessions I consider valuable. I don't want what happened in my grandmother's case to happen to me. Grandmother had six children. She had property, two apartment buildings that brought in decent money every month.

Grandmother took care of herself and her properties until the day she died. She was 87 years old. I feel like I am so much like my grandmother and still learning from her. Unlike her, however, I want to have a will. After grandmother died, the family went nuts. My two aunts got greedy and took the properties from the four brothers. My father was one of the brothers. Neither my father nor his three other brothers received a dime from the properties. I know that's not the way my grandmother would have wanted it. She loved her sons as much as she loved her two daughters.

The family is divided because of this. I have nieces

and nephews whom I love very much, and I want to leave my valuables to them. I have three homes, jewelry, and loads of great artwork. Is there a way I can write my will, or must I have a lawyer do it for me so that it would be right? Can you please tell me?

Response

I see what you mean about making sure that you have a will in place. So many times families fight over property and other valuables if the deceased does not leave a will. Many people act as if they will not die and never put things in order for their families. No one wants to think of that day. If you don't want to think of that day, then think of your family on that day. Even those that don't have many possessions should still think of making a will. You may have items that are dear to you and you want them to be preserved and passed down the family line.

Wills can be simple. All that's needed to make your will valid or accepted by the court and put into effect are the following requirements: (1) the will must be in writing. It can be hand written, typed, or printed; (2) the will must be signed with your signature at the end of the document; and (3) the will must be witnessed by at least two other people at the time of signing. They need to acknowledge they were present and must sign the will as witnessed in your presence. When all of these are in place, the court will begin the process of probate. Probate is the process of legally transferring the title of his or her property assets to the beneficiary.

It's not as complicated as you might think. And I'm sure you will enjoy your life with your nieces and nephews for many, many years to come.

Situation

44 Get That Child's Money

(Collecting Child Support)

My 24-year-old daughter had a boyfriend whom she lived with for five years. Two years ago, she had a child by him. A few months after their son was born, they broke up. For a few months, she didn't tell me he abandoned her and my grandson and that she moved into a small place. Her girlfriend went to visit her at this new place. Afterwards, she came straight to me and told me that I needed to get in touch with my daughter. My daughter was not doing well; she was struggling. I became alarmed because the girlfriend described my daughter was ashamed about how things turned out and that she was practically starving. I went over there the same day. My daughter was skin and bones and was extremely depressed. I convinced her to come home with me. I told her I would be there for her and my grandson.

I have helped her reclaim her self-esteem. I encouraged her to go back to school to get a degree. She leaves her son with me while she works part-time and attends school. I told her that the father must be held responsible and that he must pay his portion for their child. I don't know why she was reluctant to go after him. It's been two years already and now she is ready to fight for her son and make his father responsible. She sees that it is not fair to her, her son, or me. I have paid for the care of my grandson since he was three months old. I told my daughter that we would find out how to get her son's father to pay child support.

Can you tell us the exact steps to take to ensure my grandson gets his money?

Response

I certainly can tell you the steps to take. I am one that believes if you are grown enough to bring a child into this world, then you are grown enough to provide for that person who is yours. If the parent who is not taking care of the child is disabled or mentally impaired, then one can understand there may be certain challenges. Approximately 30 million children in the United States of America are owed more than $41 billion in unpaid child support, according to estimates by the Association for the Enforcement of Child Support (AECS). Since children require a lot of financial support – school, childcare, food, and a roof over their heads – if parents don't do it, then tax dollars are expended to help support them and provide Medicare.

The parents are still the ultimate responsible party. Start by getting a court order. This should happen as soon as the child is born if the parents are not married. In case of legal separation or divorce, get a court order right away! Court orders are available through the local child support agencies. These agencies can represent you, you can get an attorney, or you may represent yourself. Attorneys are usually the best way to go because they are not emotionally attached and cannot be influenced with excuses. Court orders are easy to get. You will need one if you want the father to have a legal obligation to pay child support.

Seek help through the child support enforcement agency in your area. This will ensure you are doing the best you can to collect child support for your grandson. This agency will help you collect and file the proper paperwork to ensure payment. They will collect from a non-paying parent out-of-state. The local District Attorney's Office will file the proper paperwork with the courts in the state where the non-paying parent lives and begin the process of collecting. Sometimes, you still may have to do your own detective work in locating the parent and his or her place of employment. Remember, the sooner they can be found, the faster you can get through the process. I must say that your daughter is blessed to have a Mother like you. Happiness and success to you, your daughter, and your grandson.

Situation

45 Suddenly Single
(Separation)

My husband and I have decided to separate for a while. He is an attorney and we have an eight-year-old son. Since my husband's office is close to our home, I decided to move to another city within the state. I let my son stay with my husband because I didn't want to take him out of his school. The separation was my idea. My husband wanted us to stay friends and connected because of our son. He said he was going to get an apartment for me. After he got the apartment and everything set up, he wrote up an agreement stating that it was my apartment and not his. That made me quite happy because now I can become independent.

I got a job as an assistant to a friend who is in the entertainment industry. She has always wanted me to work with her and she paid me a decent salary. My only problem is that I have no credit in my name. For the 12 years that I was married I never used my credit at all. Now, I can't really establish credit because no one will give me any.

How do I go about establishing credit with no credit?

Response

Since you are looking to establish credit for the first time, lenders can't look at your credit score to determine whether or not to lend you money. In these situations they have to examine other factors that can help them decide if you are a credit risk or not.

There are a few things you can do that can help in establishing and building your credit. The first thing you should do is open and maintain a checking and possibly even a savings account at a local bank. This is helpful in two ways:

1. When you have active bank accounts in good standing, you are proving that you can manage money. While bank accounts aren't typically a part of your credit score, lenders can use this information to determine whether or not you are a credit risk.

2. Establishing a relationship with a bank will improve your chances of obtaining a loan or a credit card through them. If you already do business with a bank, they should be the first place to look. They know you and they value your business. This existing relationship should carry some weight when seeking credit.

A Residency history: Lenders will also look to see how often you move and whether you rent or own. It pays to have a stable residence. Owning a home, even if jointly with a spouse, carries some weight as well.

Employment history: This is another important factor lenders look at to see if you can hold a job or if there are periods of unemployment. Your ability to hold a steady job can improve the likelihood of getting approved.

Utilities in your name: Even without a credit history it is possible to sign up for utilities in your own name. Having an electric or gas bill, telephone, cable, or water bill also helps. Just having your name on these accounts won't establish a credit score, but it can be helpful for first-time borrowers.

Establishing a good credit history takes time. There are no short cuts or tricks that can take you from no credit at all to a high score in a matter of months or even a few years. Your credit score is based on a number of factors such as payment history and length of time you've had credit. While it is important to initially establish credit, it is even more important to take the time to do the right thing to maintain it.

I hope you and your husband find a way back to each other for the sake of your son. In the meantime I hope that you do get the credit that you want.

101 Credit Improvement And Financial Tips

Tip # 1: Understand where credit scores come from.

Your credit scores come from the three credit bureaus -TransUnion, Experian, and Equifax. Each of these companies use different formulas to calculate your credit score. When a company is going to extend you credit, they will usually request a credit report on you from one or all of these bureaus.

Tip # 2: Enroll into a good identity theft protection program.

As you embark on the path to improving your credit scores and getting your finances straight, you want to ensure that nothing can undo what you are working hard to accomplish. Identity theft is the fastest growing crime in America, and you need to be protected.

Tip # 3: Develop an action plan for dealing with your credit score.

Improving your credit is not going to be as easy as just sending off a few letters and then magic happens. You will have to take the time to get your credit reports, analyze what is in them, how it is affecting your credit, and create a plan of attack from there.

Tip # 4: Pay your bills on time.

While it may seem that this goes without saying, it is very important to understand that your credit will greatly suffer if you make payments late. Sometimes in life late payments do happen but the later they are the worst they are. Do everything you can to avoid payments going past 60 days because that is when they become very damaging to your credit history.

Tip # 5: Avoid excessive credit.

Having a lot of credit does not do anything for your credit report other than to show that you have excessive credit that you don't use. If you do use it, make sure that you stay under 50% of your available credit on your cards because your scores will drop when you go over the 50% mark.

Tip # 6: Pay down your debts.

If your credit card balances are over 50%, you want to pay those down as quickly as possible. I recommend keeping your cards between 10% and 20% at all times. This shows the credit bureaus that you are using your credit but that you are not over-extending yourself.

Tip # 7: Have a range of credit types.

This simply means to make sure that the accounts on your credit report are not all of one type. There are two main types of accounts that will report to your credit report: (1) Revolving accounts mean you make a minimum payment every month on the balance and (2) installment accounts have a fixed payment amount each month such as a car note or a mortgage. A mix of these accounts on your report is optimal. Your credit report has other types of accounts that will report to it, but the revolving and installment are the most important when it comes to having a well rounded credit profile.

Tip # 8: Look out for identity theft.

Identity theft can affect anyone at any time, so you want to be sure that you are proactive in protecting your identity. File an identity theft report with local authorities if you even suspect something unusual going on with your credit. A specific crime does not have to be committed for you to file a police report on suspicion of identity theft. This will be very helpful to you if your identity was compromised and you need to have items suppressed on your credit report.

Tip # 9: Practice safe banking, safe computing, and safe business practices.

Bad banking practices are the perfect ways to destroy your credit report. It is very important to be wise with your identity and your finances. I do know of people who actually wrote their pin number on the back of their debit card, or they made it something very easy to figure out, such as their birthday. It may be easy to remember, but it is also easier for someone to compromise your accounts that way. I also recommend using different passwords for bank accounts than you would for your e-mail account or other Internet accounts.

Tip # 10: Check your credit score regularly.

A recent poll showed that only 15% of respondents actually had seen their credit report within the last 12 months. Checking your credit report on a regular basis is the number one way to prevent identity theft, and it will also help you know what position you are in should you decide to open up a new credit account. If your credit scores are low, you do not want to be applying for new credit because the inquiries will hurt your score even more. Know your credit report like you know yourself.

Tip # 11: Beware of debts and credit you don't use.

If you have a lot of credit on your credit report and you don't use it, that sends a message to potential creditors that they are not going to make any money off of you and unfortunately that will also lower your credit scores. If you apply for credit make sure you are going to use at least some of it because an open account that has no activity is not a good thing. If you do have an account that you are not using, request to have the credit line reduced.

Tip # 12: Be careful of inquiries on your credit report.

Every time someone looks at your credit report it can take your credit scores down. In my opinion, this is an unfair calculation to factor into your credit scores because there are so many different companies out there that are able to pull your credit report, and you have no control over this. For example, when you rent a car the car rental company will most likely pull your credit report. When you apply for a job it is likely your credit report will be pulled. The credit bureaus say that more than two inquiries in a year will hurt your credit score so you have to be very careful with putting in a lot of credit applications.

Tip # 13: Be careful of online rate comparisons.

A noted financial expert recently did an experiment on insurance rates. She got the rates for three companies online and ended up getting a better deal when she called the companies directly. Many times these online rate calculators are provided by third parties that make money when you do business through their website. The money they make represents money that could be saved if you went to the company directly. I recommend using an online quote as a guide but always talk directly to the company before you set up a policy.

Tip # 14: Don't make the mistake of thinking that you only have one credit report.

There are three credit bureaus, which means you have three separate credit reports. You will find, however, that some information on one bureau may not be present on another one. The credit bureaus do not share information, so your bank reporting to one of them does not mean that information will be on the others. Another reason why you want to check each credit report often is to be sure what is reported is accurate, and to know which companies are reporting to each bureau.

Tip # 15: Don't make the mistake of closing lots of credit accounts just to improve your score.

Never shut down an account to improve your credit scores. This will not help because the account will still show on your report and will list as "closed by consumer". If you have a lot of these items on your credit report, it is an indicator to a potential creditor that you open credit that you don't need and then close it. You do not want to give that kind of impression.

Tip # 16: Don't make quick decisions.

During the process of improving your credit score there are many decisions you will need to make. You want to make sure that your decision making is based on facts and not emotions. When you make a decision, you want to make that decision knowing exactly what the desired results are. The worst decision is a bad decision. The damage to your credit has already been done in the past so there is no need to create more damage by not making well thought out decisions. A good rule of thumb to remember is to always take a day before opening any type of long-term credit commitment. Think your decisions through with a clear head and a specific purpose in mind.

Tip # 17: Don't think having no loans or debts will improve your credit score.

In order to have a credit score, you must have credit reported to your bureau files. Do not be fooled into thinking that no credit is good credit because it is just the opposite. You will want to establish a credit score for yourself very quickly if you do not have one. Just understand that it's what you do after you get the credit that is going to really factor into your score. If you have not been able to get credit because you don't have credit then the smart way to go is with a secured credit card.

Tip # 18: Never do anything illegal to help boost your credit score.

No matter what kind of increase you get in your scores by doing something illegal the repercussions of that action will far outweigh the benefits. As you are working to improve your credit score, you will see and hear many ideas on how you might get something for nothing from fake social security numbers to buying credit cards off the Internet - there is a scammer on every corner. Don't fall for the appeal of fast results.

Tip # 19: Dispute errors on your credit report.

If you detect errors on your credit report, you have the right to dispute them. The best way to do this is by sending a letter of dispute to the appropriate credit bureau and request they remove the erroneous information or verify its accuracy.

Tip # 20: Add a note to your credit report.

You can add a comment to your credit report to explain any item on your report. Just send a consumer statement letter to the appropriate credit bureaus with the comment you want to add.

Tip # 21: Make sure you know who is looking at your credit report and why.

If you see inquiries on your credit report from companies that you don't know, you need to find out why they are pulling your credit. Typically, at the end of your credit report will be a listing of all parties who pulled your credit within a certain period of time, along with their address and phone numbers. Contact these companies to make sure you know why they pulled your report.

Tip # 22: Know the difference between soft and hard inquiries.

When you pull your credit report from a company like freecreditreport.com, it is considered a soft inquiry. A soft inquiry does have an effect on your credit score, but the impact is minimal. When you apply for credit such as a credit card or a bank loan, it is considered a hard inquiry. Hard inquiries hurt your credit more than soft ones, so be very cautious and careful with the number of inquires on your report. When buying a car, take a copy of your report with you and ask the finance manager not to submit your application to more than two lenders.

Tip # 23: Contact creditors as well as credit bureaus when correcting inaccuracies on your credit report.

Many times people make the mistake of only trying to correct errors on their credit report by communicating with the credit bureaus. This is a big mistake! You also want to communicate with the original creditor because you may be able to get information from them quicker than a credit bureau would. This information could be very helpful in correcting the mistakes on your report.

Tip # 24: Be careful where you get your online credit report - and what it contains.

There are so many commercials on TV and the radio advertising places you can get your credit report. Be careful when purchasing your credit report over the Internet, because there have been situations where people actually set up fake credit report websites just to collect peoples personal information. I recommend that you get your credit report directly from the three major credit bureaus and do not use a third-party website.

Tip # 25: If you have bad credit, establish better credit by taking out credit and repaying it quickly.

This is always a good tactic to use when improving your credit scores. It demonstrates that you are being responsible for newly approved credit lines. There are many low limit credit cards available on the market for this purpose. There are also some online catalog companies that cater to consumers looking to build or improve credit. These are also a great resource for getting small credit lines that will report to the credit bureaus. Building good credit can be easy if done wisely. Always do your research!

Tip # 26: Try secured credit if you cannot qualify for other types of credit.

Secured credit cards are a great way to establish credit because your credit line is backed with cash. Secured credit card programs you can apply for are available online. It is important to remember that secured credit cards will not automatically draft your payment from the deposit you made to open the account, so be sure to make all of your secured credit card payments by check or money order.

Tip # 27: Give it time.

Improving your credit score is not an overnight process. It probably didn't take you long to hurt your credit, but it will take some time to rebuild it. Once you begin the process of improving your credit, you must exercise patience because there are waiting periods and time frames to deal with. During the process you will not have instant favorable results, but you must stay focused on the task. No one is going to care about your credit more than you. However long it takes to improve your scores will be well worth it once you have accomplished what you set out to do.

Tip # 28: After a big financial upset, start improving your credit right away!

If you have recently suffered a divorce, bankruptcy, or any other financial setback, it is important that you immediately start to rebuild your credit. The new negative information on your report is there, but the quicker you start to have positive information added to the report, the greater your chances of improving your scores sooner rather than later. If you are using an attorney for your divorce, it is a good idea to take the cash you would spend to pay him or her and open secured credit cards. Then use the cards to pay the attorney. This way you are building credit by paying legal fees.

Tip # 29: Know the factors.

When you are considering getting involved in any type of financial transaction, you want to make sure you understand all of the factors. There are so many people who jump immediately at a deal just because they are getting what they want but end up being hurt in the long run. Make sure that you ask questions before taking a loan or any other type of financial obligation. It's easier to say "no" than to try to go back and fix what should have never been broken.

Tip # 30: Consider co-signing for loans - but consider well before taking the leap.

When you co-sign for someone else, it is important that you understand there is no difference between you and the primary in the creditor's eyes. If the primary does not pay the bill, you are going to be 100% responsible. Co-signing for other people is a dangerous proposition because you never know what could happen in their life that may cause them not to be able to honor their debt. Be very cautious when co-signing for someone else, and make sure you are willing and able to pay the debt if they cannot or will not.

Tip # 31: Don't overlook bankruptcy.

While bankruptcy should never be your first consideration when dealing with debt and credit, it is an option that can be helpful. If you are in the position that you cannot pay your bills and do not see any short-term solution, then I would recommend meeting with a qualified bankruptcy advisor to determine if this is right for you. Many people have filed bankruptcy and have recovered from it. Bankruptcy is not a death sentence, and you can overcome the negative impacts of making such a decision.

Tip # 32: Don't choose bankruptcy because someone else did.

When considering bankruptcy, you want to make sure that you are considering it for the right reasons. The right reasons for someone else may not be the same for you. Do not let anyone who is not qualified as a bankruptcy advisor convince you to make that decision if you are not 100% sure that it is the best option. Bankruptcy is a very serious step, and it is not as easy to do as it was in past years. Study the pros and cons before filing for bankruptcy. Once you start down that road you cannot come back, so it is very important to make a sound and wise decision.

Tip # 33: Learn from your mistakes.

We are all human beings, and we are going to make mistakes whether we like it or not. The worst thing you can do when you encounter financial difficulty is to take things personally and blow them out of proportion. In a perfect world every bill would be paid on time, but it's just not that way. If you make a financial mistake, don't make a bigger mistake by not learning from it. The best lesson learned is the one that doesn't have to be learned again.

Tip # 34: Seek professional help.

It is a reality of life that sometimes people just can't handle financial problems on their own. If you find yourself in trouble and can't work things out on your own, the smartest move you can make is to seek out professional help. There are many credit counseling agencies and professionals who can help you through your situation, but no one can help you if you don't ask for it.

Tip # 35: Look out for credit repair companies.

Credit repair does not work! We talked earlier in this book about how if your car is taken to the shop and only some of the problems are fixed, then what you get back is not a repaired car. Do not be fooled by credit repair companies that claim they can fix your problems overnight, and also make grand promises. The reason so many people are taken advantage of by credit repair scams is their willingness to believe anything they are told. If someone makes credit repair promises, have them show you documentation that proves they have made good on their promises to others. The best recommendation is to work on improving your own credit and do not turn your problems over to people you don't know and may not be able to trust.

Tip # 36: Seek free self-help before paying someone for credit repair services.

There are many nonprofit agencies that can help you in your attempts to solve some of your debt and credit problems. There are many inexpensive solutions on the market that will help you work on improving your own credit. The recommended solution is a software program called Capital Credit XP: Personal Credit Improvement Software. This software only costs $39.95 and will allow you to work on the credit of two people. You can download the software from the situations101.com website.

Tip # 37: It will be easier for financial experts to help you if you seek help sooner rather than later.

If you see a small fire in your living room are you going to wait to call the fire department only after it becomes a big fire and threatens to destroy the entire house? Or are you going to move quickly? The common sense answer is to move quickly, and it is the same with your credit report. If your credit report is starting to suffer and you need help, get help now. Waiting will only make things worse. The best results will come from your taking immediate action.

Tip # 38: Be honest.

Earlier in this book we talked about a credit repair scam using CPN or credit protection numbers. Never use any credit improvement technique that involves dishonesty on credit applications. Nothing good will ever come out of it. If you lie on a credit application you are committing a very serious crime that could land you in jail.

Tip # 39: Your bank has good and reliable credit information.

Unfortunately, this is more of a myth than a reality. While banks function and revolve around the credit industry, each bank has its own way of looking at different possibilities and are in business to sell you one of their products or services. It is recommended that you always use a third-party, unbiased source when making banking and financial related decisions.

Tip # 40: Learn to budget.

You cannot drive from one place to another if you don't know the directions. The same applies to a budget for your home. A budget is a road map to financial success.

Tip # 41: Live within your means.

Live within your means is a concept that simply calls for you to make smart decisions about finances. It does not make sense to buy a car that will cost you $1000 a month if you only make $2000 a month on your job. If you really want that car, make the decision to create more means so you can afford it.

Tip # 42: Get out of the spending habit.

There are many upscale discount and bargain stores where you can shop instead of always going to the most expensive store in the mall. What you don't spend today, you will have saved for tomorrow.

Tip # 43: Save.

Saving money is a very important skill that, unfortunately, most Americans do not practice. You have to understand that once you have spent it, it is gone. If you don't have a way to make it back, then do without it. That may not mean much when everything is normal, but in the event of an unforeseen circumstance or emergency, the money in a savings account can truly prove to be a lifesaver.

Tip # 44: Keep track of your money.

Failure to keep track of where your money is going is a bad habit if you ever plan on achieving financial stability. Always keep track of your money by managing your checkbook and your accounts to make sure that you are in touch with your finances.

Tip # 45: Take out one luxury expense and save!

The average cable television bill runs between $40 and $100 a month. Just think how much money that would be over a 10-year period of time if you did not have the cable package that offers all of the movie channels. Find one small luxury in your life that is costing you, and make the decision to let that pleasure go for one year, and see how much money you're able to keep in the bank.

Tip # 46: Build assets and capital.

Just because you don't have a lot, does not mean you're not worth a lot! However, when it comes to banking that seems to be a harsh reality. It is very difficult, many times, to get the types of loans or credit lines that you need if you don't have any assets to use as collateral.

Tip # 47: Find more than one avenue to generate income.

There are only 24 hours in a day, but that doesn't mean that you can't do multiple things with those 24 hours. The key to financial success in America is to be diversified. Many people have found themselves laid off from a job and in a bad position because they didn't have alternative means to supplement their income. I suggest getting involved in a good network marketing company or some other type of low cost venture that can create a secondary income for you.

Tip # 48: Prepare for financial emergencies.

You never need it until you need it, but when you do, it is good to have it. Hopefully there will never be crisis or emergencies that show up in your life, but if they do, they can be a lot worse if you are financially unprepared for them. Financial emergencies may occur, so it is always good to set aside a small portion of each paycheck for those emergencies.

Tip # 50: Get insurance.

Always make sure you have insurance for your car, your home, and your health. You don't need it until you need it!

Tip # 51: Have a lawyer go over all your business contracts.

It may be okay to take an over-the-counter remedy for a cold but it is not okay to perform open-heart surgery on yourself. Any time you do business make sure you have agreements in place that will serve your purpose. Many small business owners get into trouble because they do handshake business. Handshake business is good when everything goes right but when things go wrong you are going to want to be in the strongest position. Always protect the things you have worked hard for in business by making the investment in good legal assistance.

Tip # 52: Know how money works.

Money is a funny thing because it has so many different facets. It is important to understand how money works when it relates to your life and your lifestyle. Remember, no one is going to take your money as seriously as you will. Make sure that you have the proper understanding as to how it works and how to make it work for you. The average consumer spends more time watching TV than they do managing their money. Take the time to understand what you need to know about your money.

Tip # 53: Take care of other things besides a credit score that will affect how lenders view you.

Just because you have a high credit score does not mean you are going to get approved for all the credit you apply for. In this economy, many people are declined for credit even though their scores are strong. You always want to take care of other financial aspects such as assets, collateral, and strong financial statements. Usually, the more money you are requesting, the larger the number of requirements needed for approval. Make sure you stay on top of everything!

Tip # 54: Follow up on closed accounts.

There have been so many situations where people thought an account was closed and it never was. This can hurt their credit score. Never take it for granted that an account was actually closed. If you close an account, call the company at least 30 to 45 days later to confirm the account was closed.

Tip # 55: Don't move around a lot.

If you do move a lot make sure that you are constantly updating your creditors to show them you are responsible and a good communicator.

Tip # 56: Assemble good team to help with your credit score.

Do your research and your homework before making the decision to team up with any credit improvement company or law firm. We recommend using Lexington Law (www.lexingtonlaw.com) if you do not have the time or desire to work on your own credit.

Tip # 57: Avoid switching credit card companies and credit accounts too often.

This also goes along with the concept of presenting stability to a creditor. Anything on your credit report that suggests that you are not stable will cause a potential creditor to be less willing to extend credit to you.

Tip # 58: Keep your records up to date.

It doesn't make any sense to have financial records if they are not up to date. Make sure you keep your checkbook balanced and your tax returns up to date. You don't ever want to be caught in a position where you are inconvenienced because you do not have access to current information.

Tip # 59: Always be sure that your creditors know your current address.

The worst thing in the world you can do is to make someone who has loaned you money or extended credit to you feel like you are hiding from them. If you move, it is important to make sure that your creditors know how to reach you.

Tip # 60: Talk to lenders and creditors in tough times.

Many people are apprehensive and nervous about talking to their creditors when payments may be late. The best thing you can do with a creditor is to maintain goodwill with them. A lot of times creditors can adjust payment dates and even work out other payment arrangements if they are aware of your situation.

Tip # 61: Ask your creditor and bank to waive fees.

You have not because you ask not! You always have the right to ask that your creditors and your bank remove certain fees and charges from your account(s). Remember they need you to stay in business more than you need them. Don't be afraid to ask for what you need.

Tip # 62: Stay financially organized.

Organization is the key to accessing information when you need it. No one wants to be the target of a tax audit, but if that happens, you will go through a lot less trouble if your paperwork is well organized. If you are not a good organizer, hire an organization specialist to help you get started.

Tip # 63: Set short-term goals and frequent credit self-checks in order to track your progress.

You have to know what your benchmarks are, and you have to be willing to go back and evaluate the progress you are making as you work to improve your credit and your financial situation. Stay on top of it.

Tip # 64: Take care of the details when applying for credit.

If you are going to fill out a credit application, make sure that you take the time to fill it out properly. The smallest oversight, such as a transposed phone number, can be the very thing to cause a credit application to be denied. Take your time and pay attention when applying for credit.

Tip # 65: Don't make the mistake of thinking that small differences in credit scores or loan interest rates won't make a big impact.

This is a mistake that is made by so many and it costs them dearly. You have to understand how interest rates work to make a good decision. In some instances a simple increase of 1% on an interest rate can cost you thousands of dollars over a period of time. If you do not understand how interest will affect your transaction, then you are not ready to do that transaction. Ask questions and make sure you know what you are getting into.

Tip # 66: If you need to improve your credit, stay organized with a to-do list that ensures you won't forget anything.

The worst thing in the world to do when improving your credit is to get all the accounts off your report except for one because you forgot about it. Stay organized and make sure that you follow a to-do list and that you are not haphazard in your approach. It is always good to take notes when you are talking to creditors and make a new to-do list based on those conversations. Being consistent is the key to getting good results.

Tip # 67: Automate your finances.

Software was created to help make our lives easier and more efficient. The days of managing your finances with a pen and paper are long gone, and it is important that you understand the technology that can help you be a better manager of your finances. With programs on the market such as Quicken and Microsoft Money, you can take control of your finances and get a great education in the process by using the resources that are available to you. If you are unsure of what software you need to manage your finances you can ask any CPA or financial advisor for help.

Tip # 68: Refinance loans.

Sometimes you have to take a bad deal just to get started, but that doesn't mean you have to live with that bad deal forever. The whole concept of refinancing is so you can do better than you did at first. Even if your credit scores are not perfect, do not accept your current situation without at least exploring opportunities to lower interest rates and shorten payment terms. If you are going to refinance, your credit scores are going to be very important, so make sure you know your scores before seeking a refinance.

Tip # 69: Look for loans that are offered for bad credit risks.

There are many companies out there that will extend credit to you even if your credit scores are low. I do caution you, however, to be careful because some of these companies are predators looking for people they can take advantage of. Just because someone will approve you does not mean that it's in your best interest to accept the credit. If you come across an offer that seems too good to be true - it probably is. Don't take anything you find without knowing all of the details. It is much easier to stay out of a bad deal than it is to get out of one.

Tip # 70: Always know your credit score before speaking to lenders.

This is especially important when it comes to buying a car. If you walk into a car dealership and you do not know your credit scores, it is very likely that you will not leave that dealership with the best deal. Make sure you understand what is on your credit report and what that means to a potential creditor because that will be the power you need when negotiating a deal.

Tip # 71: Consider speaking to lenders face-to-face if you have a low credit score.

Even though computers make most of the decisions in banking and credit extension these days, it never hurts to sit down with your banker. You never know what a little relationship can do for you and what you are trying to accomplish. We are not saying that a banker is going to give you money just because you're a nice person, but there have been many instances where personal influence has helped people secure financing. With a personal perspective on what you are trying to do, a good banker can be a great advocate for you when working to get you approved for a loan.

Tip # 72: Don't let a low credit score make you swear off purchases you must make.

If you need a car - buy a car. If you need a credit card - get a credit card. Do not let bad credit deter you. There are many people with bad credit, but that does not mean they do not deserve those things that will make their lives easier. Just understand that your bad credit means you may pay more than you would if you had good credit.

Tip # 73: Make arrangements to pay your bills when you are on vacation.

There have been so many instances when someone has been away, especially if they were in the military, and their credit scores suffered because they did not make arrangements to have their bills paid. There are services that will manage the payment of your bills if you are going to be out of the country or away for a long period of time. This is also good advice for anyone who may have to serve jail or prison time. Just because you are in trouble with the law does not mean that you should let your credit suffer.

Tip # 74: Consider online banking or telephone banking to make paying bills easier and more efficient.

Paying bills in the Internet age is much easier because it can be automated for you. As long as you have the money in your account, there are online bill paying programs that will automatically generate payments as bills are issued. I highly recommend enrolling into automatic bill paying programs, especially when it comes to payment on accounts that will report to the credit bureaus.

Tip # 75: Simplify your bills.

This is very easy to do especially when it comes to home phone service, Internet service, and television service. There was a time when these three services came from three different companies, but now many providers offer multiple services, and it is best to use them because they will save you money.

Tip # 76: Pay your bills as soon as you get them.

If you can do this, it is the best advice in the world. If you cannot do this, make sure you pay your bills as soon as you possibly can. You do not want to get in the habit of paying bills only when you get a disconnect notice. The fees, penalties and re-connection fees are usually very high.

Tip # 77: Set aside a regular day, time, and place for paying bills.

Paying bills is an important part of your financial lifestyle, and you have to make the time and effort to get it done. Many people get behind on bills just because they forget to take care of them. Do not let yourself be in that situation because at some point your credit score will suffer.

Tip # 78: Record your financial duties on a calendar - just like all your other appointments.

Manage financial time the same way you manage everything else. There is nothing wrong with having a specific date and time on your schedule to take care of financial responsibilities. Whether it's going to the bank and setting up a new bank account or balancing your checkbook, you want to make sure that you stay on top of your financial duties.

Tip # 79: Use the web.

The Internet is a technology that levels the playing field. There are so many online resources available you should be knowledgeable of those things you need to know. You cannot learn everything at one time, but over the course of time you can greatly expand your financial knowledge.

Tip # 80: If you are a student, do not take the first credit card offered to you.

Rule # 1 - Always turn down the first one. Rule # 2 - Think about the second one.

Tip # 81: Never let friends use your credit card.

As a student, this is one of the worst things you can do. There will be times when a good friend may need a little money or may need a little help, but you cannot use your credit card for that purpose. If you want to give them some cash, that is fine, but buying gas and groceries on your credit card to help out a friend is not a good move. You don't want to put your credit in jeopardy over a kind gesture to a friend.

Tip # 82: Do everything you can to pay for education through means other than loans.

Student loans can be a blessing and a curse all at the same time. They are a blessing because they will help you finance your education, but they can be a curse if you remain unemployed for any length of time after you get out of school. I always tell people to finance their own education through part-time jobs or by borrowing from friends and family members as opposed to borrowing from the bank. There are also grant programs and special assistance programs you can look into as well. Just be sure to know what you are looking for before you get started in your search. There is a lot out there - don't waste time.

Tip # 83: Never default on a student loan.

Don't do it! It will haunt you forever! In many ways, not paying on student loans is worse than never paying your taxes. There are many financial repercussions that can show up in your life because you have unpaid student loans. If you can avoid taking a student loan, you should, but if you cannot, make sure that you do not default on that loan.

Tip # 84: Save money by taking advantage of student discounts.

There are many student discount programs out there, but you have to be willing to take the time to do the research, and take advantage of those opportunities.

Tip # 85: Follow the "cash for wants, loans for needs" rule.

If you want it and can't buy it with cash, don't get it. This is the best advice for a student because they can very easily get into credit trouble by using credit cards for purchases such as shoes, clothes, and relationship needs. All credit card charges incur interest, so you are really paying more for what you buy. Be smart from the start. Respect your credit because once it's damaged, it can be very hard to fix.

Tip # 86: Make learning about money a priority.

Unfortunately, the percentage of Americans that are financially literate is very low. Learning about money is very important, and it should be taught in the home at a very young age. You can never know too much about money, and the more you know the better off you will be. Take time each month to read a financial magazine, a financial advice book, or even watch a financial television show to lean about saving, investing and other financial matters. What you don't know can hurt you. It is never too late to learn.

Tip # 87: Start building credit early - and do it well.

Being afraid of credit is not good. Credit is not designed to hurt you. In fact, it is there to help you. When credit is misunderstood, serious problems occur in your life. Building credit at an early age is a wise decision, but you have to remember the foundation created must be sustained. Always respect he credit you established. It is there for building and not abusing. You also do not need to blow through your credit and pay it off quickly because that does not show consistency. Take your time and do things small, but often.

Tip # 88: Consolidate your loans to make repayment easier.

If you find you are writing five or six checks a month to pay on credit card debts and loans, you may want to consider some type of consolidation program. A consolidation program will help you streamline your debt repayment process, and it will also help to improve your credit scores. When considering a consolidation program, don't forget to do your homework on each program. They are all different and you need to make sure you get the one works best for you.

Tip # 89: Pay down your debts by making larger than minimal payments.

If you are only making minimum payments on your credit card debt, then you are hurting yourself in two ways. The first is because you could be paying the maximum amount of interest payments on that debt. The second is because you are minimizing the amount of available credit you have in case of emergencies. It is highly recommended that you pay at least three times your minimum payment every month. That will eliminate the debt much quicker and help you build your credit at the same time.

Tip # 90: If you are financing a car, consider a larger down payment in order to take out a smaller loan.

Many times, finance managers at car dealerships will ask you how much of a note you want to pay. Remember, the finance manager is not going to be the one paying your monthly payment, so don't take their advice on maintaining a low note. They are there to sell a car. You are there to get the best deal. Control your note with a larger down payment.

Tip # 91: As a student, it is always a good idea to work a side job to make extra money.

Take on some type of part-time job so you can have the experience of earning your own money and managing your own financial affairs.

Tip # 92: Be cautious of payday loans.

There are many instances where a payday loan may become necessary, but you want to make sure that it is absolutely necessary. Payday loans are designed to take advantage of your need for money. Payday loan companies can make life a living hell for people that do not repay the loans on time. Be sure that you are not shooting yourself in the foot by taking a payday loan you really don't need.

Tip # 93: Do not use one debt to repay another.

This is the infamous concept of using Visa to pay MasterCard. If you are in the process of building credit, then paying on one credit card or loan with another one is okay, but you need to be wise in this practice. If you are going to use debt to pay debt, then make sure you have an exit strategy that will allow you to eliminate doing so.

Tip # 94: Give yourself a break.

There is no point in beating yourself up over your credit score. Instead, promise yourself that you will do better in the future, and then work to improve your credit rather than berating yourself.

Tip # 95: Don't make excuses.

If you did things in the past to hurt your credit, just admit to yourself that it was a mistake and don't try to make excuses. Lenders are usually willing to work with you, but no one wants to hear that every single item on your credit report is there due to no fault of your own. No one's luck is that bad. Just own up to your mistakes - no matter what.

Tip # 96: Give yourself a treat - without affecting your credit rating.

Enjoy life! It is okay to take a little bit of money and spend on yourself, even while you are in the process of rebuilding your credit. Don't let your experiences from the past create a dark cloud over your present and future.

Tip # 97: Work on your emotional response to debt and money.

Don't be so quick to react as if the house is on fire. With time and a little patience, the right financial decision can always be reached.

Tip # 98: Learn to deal with collection agencies.

We have all heard many stories about how much of a pain in the "you know what" collection agencies can be. Collection agencies may resort to some devious tactics that are unfair, but they are calling you for a reason. If you are in the process of communicating with a collection agency, you need to remember to not take it personal or allow yourself to get frustrated. If you do not have the money to pay them, just be honest.

Tip # 99: Do not make promises that you know you can't keep.

No matter what you owe, do not let any collection agent back you into a corner that you cannot get out of. Always take control of the situation and don't let them bully you.

Tip # 100: Stay focused.

If managed properly, tough financial times can turn out to be a great place to learn some very good lessons for the future. If you are going to be successful, you are going to endure some financial challenges. Don't lose focus of the bigger picture.

Tip # 101: Keep at it.

Never give up on what you are trying to accomplish when it comes to improving your credit. A good attitude and a positive outlook will take you much further than if you let your situation keep you negative and unhappy. Bad credit happens to people from all walks of life. What happened in the past is in the past, and now it's time to focus on the present and the future.

Good luck and best wishes!

101 Financial Terms Every American Should Know

1. **1/1 ARM:** An adjustable-rate mortgage has a set initial interest rate for the first year. After that period, the mortgage rate adjusts each year. Each annual rate adjustment is based on (or "indexed to") another rate, often the yield on a U.S. Treasury note.

2. **10/1 ARM:** An adjustable-rate mortgage that has a set initial interest rate for the first 10 years. After that period, the mortgage rate adjusts each year.

3. **3/1 Interest-Only ARM:** An adjustable rate mortgage in which none of the payments go toward paying off the loan principal for the first three years.

4. **3-in-1 Credit Report:** Also called a merged credit report, this type of report includes your credit data from TransUnion, Equifax and Experian in a side-by-side format for easy comparison.

5. **Adjustable Rate Mortgage (ARM):** A home loan where the interest rate is changed periodically based on a standard financial index. ARM's offer lower initial interest rates with the risk of rates increasing in the future. In comparison, a fixed rate mortgage (FRM's) offers a higher rate that will not change for the length of the loan. ARMs often have caps on how much the interest rate can rise or fall.

6. **Alternative Mortgage:** Any home loan that is not a standard fixed-rate mortgage. This includes ARM's, reverse mortgages and jumbo mortgages.

7. **Amortization:** The process of gradually repaying a debt with regularly scheduled payments over a period of time.

8. **Annual Percentage Rate (APR):** The interest rate being charged on a debt, expressed as a yearly rate. Credit cards often have several different APR's - one for purchases, one for cash advances and one for balance transfers.

9. **Application Scoring:** A specific kind of statistical scoring that businesses use to evaluate an applicant for acceptance or denial. Similar to credit scoring, application scoring often factors in other relevant details such as employment status and income to determine risk.

10. **Appraised Value:** An educated opinion of how much a property is worth. An appraiser considers the price of similar homes in the area, the condition of the home and the features of the property to estimate the value.

11. **Authorized User:** Anyone who uses your credit cards or credit accounts with your permission. More specifically, someone who has a credit card from your account with their name on it. An authorized user is not legally responsible for the debt.

12. **Back-End Ratio or Back Ratio:** The sum of your monthly mortgage payment and all other monthly debts (credit cards, car payments, student loans, etc.) divided by your monthly pre-tax income. Traditionally, lenders wouldn't give people loans that increased this ratio past 36%, but they often do now.

13. **Balance Transfer:** The process of moving all or part of the outstanding balance on one credit card to another account. Credit card companies often offer special rates for balance transfers.

14. **Balloon Payment:** A loan where the payments don't pay off the principal in full by the end of the term. When the loan term expires (usually after 5-7 years), the borrower must pay a balloon payment for the remaining amount or refinance. Balloon loans sometimes include convertible options that allow the remaining amount to automatically be transferred into a long-term mortgage.

15. **Beacon Score:** The name of the FICO score from Equifax. There are thousands of slightly different credit scoring formulas used by bankers, lenders, creditors, insurers and retailers.

16. **Broker Premium:** The amount a mortgage broker is paid for serving as the middleman between a lender and a borrower. This premium comes from the surcharge a broker applies to a discounted loan before offering it to a borrower.

17. **Cash-Out Refinance:** A new mortgage for an existing property in which the amount borrowed is greater than the amount of the previous mortgage. The difference is given to the borrower in cash when the loan is closed.

18. **Charge-Off:** When a creditor or lender writes off the balance of a delinquent debt, no longer expecting it to be repaid. A charge-off is also known as a bad debt.

19. **ChexSystems:** A credit reporting company that tracks your banking history and provides this data to banks when you apply for a new checking account. Negative records, such as bounced checks, can be kept in their database for up to five years.

20. **Closing Costs:** The amounts charged to a consumer when they are transferring ownership or borrowing against a property. Closing costs include lender, title and escrow fees and usually range from 3-6% of the purchase price.

21. **Collections:** When a business sells your debt for a reduced amount to an agency in order to recover the amounts owed. Credit card debts, medical bills, cell phone bills, utility charges, library fees and video store fees are often sold to collections. Collection agencies attempt to recover past-due debts by contacting the borrower via phone and mail. Collection records can remain on your credit report for 7 years from the last 180 day late payment on the original debt. Your rights are defined by the Fair Debt Collection Practices Act.

22. **Combined Loan-to-Value Ratio:** The total amount you are borrowing in mortgage debts divided by the home's fair market value. Someone with a $50,000 first mortgage and a $20,000 equity line secured against a $100,000 house would have a CLTV ratio of 70%.

23. **Convenience Check:** Checks provided by your credit card company that you can use to access your available credit. These checks often have different rates and terms than your standard credit card charges.

24. **Convertible ARM**: An adjustable rate mortgage that can be converted to a fixed-rate mortgage under specified conditions.

25. **Credit Obligation:** An agreement where a person becomes legally responsible for paying back borrowed money. This does include joint accounts as well as accounts that the individual is acting as a cosigner or personal guarantee on a business credit account.

26. **Credit Score:** A numerical evaluation of your credit history used by businesses to quickly understand how risky a borrower you are. Credit scores are calculated using complex mathematical formulas that look at your most current payment history, debts, credit history, inquiries and other factors from your credit report. Credit scores usually range from 300-850, the higher the score, the better.

27. **Debt Consolidation:** A process of combining debts into one loan or repayment plan. Debt consolidation can be done on your own, with a financial institution or through a counseling service. Student loans are often consolidated in order to secure a lower interest rate.

28. **Debt Settlement Assistance:** A process where you pay an agency to negotiate directly with your creditors in the hopes of making significantly reduced settlements for your debts. Working with a debt settlement company can result in damaged credit from numerous late payments and collection records. Consumers should fully investigate the practices and costs of working with a debt settlement company before signing up.

29. **Debt-to-Income Ratio:** The percentage of your monthly pre-tax income that is used to pay off debts such as auto loans, student loans and credit card balances. Lenders look at two ratios: The front-end ratio is the percentage of monthly pre-tax earnings that are spent on house payments. The back-end ratio is where the borrower's other debts are factored in along with the house payments.

30. **Empirica Score:** A cosigner is legally responsible for the loan and the shared account will appear on their credit report.

31. **Equal Credit Opportunity Act (ECOA):** A law that protects consumers from discrimination on the basis of race, sex, public assistance income, age, marital status, nationality or religion in the credit and lending process.

32. **Expiration Term:** The set number of years that a record will remain on your credit report as mandated by the FCRA. Most negative records stay on your credit report for 7-10 years. The shortest expiration term is two years for inquiry records. The longest expiration term is 15 years for paid tax liens or indefinitely for unpaid tax liens. Positive information can also stay on your credit report indefinitely.

33. **Fair and Accurate Credit Transaction (FACT) Act:** The FACT Act was signed into law December 2003 and includes several consumer credit industry regulations. This law requires credit bureaus to provide all US residents with a free copy of their credit report once every 12 months. The law also includes new privacy regulations, identity theft protections and dispute procedure requirements.

34. **Fair Credit Reporting Act:** The Fair Credit Reporting Act (FCRA) is a United States federal law (codified at 15 U.S.C. § 1681 et seq.) that regulates the collection, dissemination, and use of consumer information, including consumer credit information.

35. **The Fair Debt Collection Practices Act (FDCPA),:** 15 U.S.C. § 1692 et seq., is a United States statute added

in 1978 as Title VIII of the Consumer Credit Protection Act. Its purposes are to eliminate abusive practices in the collection of consumer debts, to promote fair debt collection, and to provide consumers with an avenue for disputing and obtaining validation of debt information in order to ensure the information's accuracy. The Act creates guidelines under which debt collectors may conduct business, defines rights of consumers involved with debt collectors, and prescribes penalties and remedies for violations of the Act.

36. **Fannie Mae:** The largest mortgage investor. A government-sponsored enterprise that buys mortgages from lenders, bundles them into investments and sells them on the secondary mortgage market. Formerly known as the Federal National Mortgage Association.

37. **File Freeze:** Consumers can request that the credit bureaus freeze their credit reports. This freeze stops new credit from being issued in your name by blocking creditors, lenders, insurers and other companies from accessing your credit data. In some cases, a $10 fee for each credit bureau is required to process the file freeze. The freeze can also be temporarily or permanently undone for an additional fee.

38. **Finance Charge:** The total cost of using credit. Besides interest charges, the finance charge may include other costs such as cash-advance fees.

39. **Fixed-Rate Option:** A home equity line of credit financing option that allows borrowers to specify the payments and interest on a portion of their balance. This can be done a few times during the life of the loan, usually for an additional fee.

40. **Fixed Rate Mortgage (FRM):** A mortgage with an interest rate that remains constant for the entire duration of the loan. FRM's have longer terms (15-30 years) and higher interest rates than adjustable rate mortgages but are not at risk for increasing interest rates.

41. **Foreclosure:** When a borrower is in default on a loan or mortgage, the creditor can enact a legal process to claim ownership of the collateral property. Foreclosure usually involves a forced sale of the property where the proceeds go toward paying off the debt.

42. **Fraud Alert:** If you suspect that you are a victim of identity theft, you may contact the credit bureaus to request

that a 90-day fraud alert is placed on your credit reports. If you have been a victim of identity theft you only need to contact one bureau to have a temporary 90 day alert added to all three of your credit reports. This 90-day alert notifies potential creditors that your identity may have been stolen and suggests that they take extra steps to confirm your identity before opening a new account. If it turns out that your identity has been stolen, you can request an extended 7 year alert by providing documentation of the crime (such as a police report).

43. **Freddie Mac:** Formerly known as the Federal Home Loan Mortgage Corporation, this is a government-sponsored firm that buys mortgages from lenders, pools them with other loans and sells them to investors.

44. **Garnishment:** When a creditor receives legal permission to take a portion of your assets (bank account, salary, etc) to repay a delinquent debt.

45. **Ginnie Mae:** Also known as the Government National Mortgage Association. A part of the Department of Housing and Urban Development that buys mortgages from lending institutions and pools them to form securities, which it then sells to investors.

46. **Grace Period:** A period of time, often about 25 days, during which you can pay your credit card bill without incurring a finance charge. With most credit card accounts, the grace period applies only if you pay your balance in full each month. It does not apply if you carry a balance forward or in the case of cash advances. If your account has no grace period, interest will be charged on a purchase as soon as it is made.

47. **Hard Inquiry:** A record of a business request to see your credit report data for the purpose of an application for credit. Hard inquiries appear on your credit report each time you complete an application for a credit card, loan, cell phone, etc. Hard inquiries remain on your credit report for 2 years but are only included in your credit score for the first 12 months.

48. **High-LTV Equity Loan:** A specific kind of home loan that causes your loan-to-value ratio to be 125% or more. When the total principal of a loan leaves the borrower with debt that exceeds the fair market value of the home, the interest paid on the portion of the loan above that value may not be tax deductible.

49. **Home Equity:** The part of a home's value that the mortgage borrower owns outright. This is the difference between the fair market value of the home and the principal balances of all mortgage loans.

50. **Home Ownership and Equity Protection Act:** A law designed to discourage predatory lending in mortgages and home equity loans.

51. **Housing Expense Ratio:** The percentage of your monthly pre-tax income that goes toward your house payment. The general rule is that this ratio shouldn't exceed 28%. This is also known as the "front ratio."

52. **Inquiry:** A record on your credit report that shows every time you, one of your creditors, or a potential creditor requests a copy of your credit report data.

53. **Installment Account:** A type of loan where the borrower makes the same payment each month. This includes personal loans and automotive loans. Mortgage loans are also installment accounts but are usually classified by the credit reporting system as real-estate accounts instead.

54. **Installment Agreement Adjustment:** An agreement where the borrower commits to making fixed payments on an account that are different from the amount originally agreed to when account was opened.

55. **Interest Rate:** A measure of the cost of credit, expressed as a percent. For variable-rate credit card plans, the interest rate is explicitly tied to another interest rate. The interest rate on fixed-rate credit card plans, though not explicitly tied to changes in other interest rates, can also change over time.

56. **Interest Rate Cap:** A limit on how much a borrower's percentage rate can increase or decrease at rate adjustment periods and over the life of the loan. Interest rate caps are used for Adjustable Rate Mortgage ARM loans where the rates can vary at certain points.

57. **Interest:** The money a borrower pays for the ability to borrow from a lender or creditor. Interest is calculated as a percentage of the money borrowed and is paid over a specified time.

58. **Interest-Only Loan:** A type of loan where the repayment only covers the interest that accumulates on the loan balance and not the actual price of the property. The principal does not decrease with the payments.

59. **Introductory Rate:** A temporary, low interest rate offered on a credit card in order to attract customers. Under the CARD Act, an introductory rate must remain in effect for a minimum of 6 months before converting to a normal or variable rate.

60. **Judgment:** A decision from a judge on a civil action or lawsuit; usually an amount of money a person is required to pay to satisfy a debt or a penalty. Judgment records remain on your credit report for 7 years and harm your credit score significantly.

61. **Late Payment Charge:** A fee charged by your creditor or lender when your payment is made after the date due. Late payment charges usually range from $10-50.

62. **Lien:** A legal claim against a person's property, such as a car or a house, as security for a debt. A lien (pronounced "lean") may be placed by a contractor who did work on your house or a mechanic who repaired your car and didn't get paid. The property cannot be sold without paying the lien. Tax liens can remain on your credit report indefinitely if left unpaid or for 15 years from the date paid.

63. **Loan Origination Fee:** A fee charged by a lender for underwriting a loan. The fee is often expressed in "points;" a point is 1% of the loan amount.

64. **Loan Processing Fee:** A fee charged by a lender for accepting a loan application and gathering the supporting paperwork.

65. **Loan-to-Value Ratio (LTV):** The percentage of a home's price that is financed with a loan. On a $100,000 home, if the buyer makes a $20,000 down payment and borrows $80,000, the loan-to-value ratio is 80%. When refinancing a mortgage, the LTV ratio is calculated using the appraised value of the home, not the sale price.

66. **Low-Down Mortgages:** Secured loans that require a small down payment, usually less than 10%. Often, low-down mortgages are offered to special kinds of borrowers such as first-time buyers, police officers, veterans, etc. These kinds of loans sometimes require that private mortgage insurance (PMI) is purchased by the borrower.

67. **Mortgage Banker:** A person or company that originates home loans, sells them to investors (such as Fannie Mae) and processes monthly payments.

68. **Mortgage Interest Expense:** A tax term for the interest paid on a loan that is fully deductible, up to certain limits, when you itemize income taxes.

69. **Mortgage Refinance:** The process of paying off and replacing an old loan with a new mortgage. Borrowers usually choose to refinance a mortgage to get a lower interest rate, lower their monthly payments, avoid a balloon payment or to take cash out of their equity.

70. **Negative Amortization:** When your minimum payment toward a debt is not enough to cover the interest charges. When this occurs, your debt balance continues to increase despite your payments.

71. **Opt-Out:** You can opt-out from pre-approved credit card offers, insurance offers and other third party marketing offers or solicitations by calling 1-888-5-OPT-OUT. Calling this number will stop mail offers that use your credit data from all three credit bureaus.

72. **Over-Limit Fee:** A fee charged by a creditor when your spending exceeds the credit limit set on your card, usually $10-50. Under the CARD Act, credit card issuers must first get your consent before charging over-limit fees.

73. **PAYDEX® Score:** Dun & Bradstreet's unique dollar-weighted numerical indicator of how a business paid its bills over the past year, based on trade experiences reported to D&B by various vendors. The D&B PAYDEX Score ranges from 1 to 100, with higher scores indicating better payment performance.

74. **Periodic Rate:** The interest rate you are charged each billing period. For most credit cards, the periodic rate is a monthly rate. You can calculate your card's periodic rate by dividing the APR by 12. A credit card with an 18% APR has a monthly periodic rate of 1.5%.

75. **Permissible Purpose:** Specific guidelines regulating when your credit data can be reviewed and by what type of business. These guidelines are part of the FCRA laws under Section 604.

76. **PITI:** Acronym for the four elements of a mortgage payment: principal, interest, taxes and insurance.

77. **Point:** A unit for measuring fees related to a loan; a point equals 1% of a mortgage loan. Some lenders charge "origination points" to cover the expense of making a loan. Some borrowers pay "discount points" to reduce the loan's interest rate.

78. **Prepayment Penalty:** A fee that a lender charges a borrower who pays off their loan before the end of its scheduled term. Prepayment penalties are not charged by most standard lenders. Sub prime borrowers should review the terms of their loan carefully to see if this fee is included.

79. **Principal:** The amount of money borrowed with a loan or the amount of money owed, excluding interest.

80. **Private Mortgage Insurance (PMI):** A form of insurance that protects the lender by paying the costs of a foreclosure on a house if the borrower stops paying the loan. Private mortgage insurance usually is required if the down payment is less than 20% of the sale price.

81. **Qualifying Ratios:** As calculated by lenders, the percentage of income that is spent on housing debt and combined household debt.

82. **Rate Shopping:** Applying for credit with several lenders to find the best interest rate, usually for a mortgage or a car loan. If done within a short period of time, such as two weeks, it should have little impact on a person's credit score.

83. **Reaffirmation Agreement:** An agreement by a bankrupt debtor to continue paying a dischargeable debt after the bankruptcy, usually to keep collateral or a mortgaged property that would otherwise be repossessed.

84. **Re-aging Accounts:** A process where a creditor can roll-back an account record with the credit bureaus. This is commonly used when cardholders request that late payment records be removed because they are incorrect or are the results of a special circumstance. However, re-aging can also be used illegally by collections agencies to make a debt account appear much younger than it actually is. Some collection agencies use this tactic to keep an account from expiring from your credit report in order to get you to pay the debt.

85. **Reverse Mortgage:** A mortgage that allows elderly borrowers to access their equity without selling their home. The lender makes payments to the borrower with a reverse mortgage. The loan is repaid from the proceeds of the estate when the borrower moves or passes away.

86. **Revolving Account:** An account where your balance and monthly payment can fluctuate. Most credit cards are revolving accounts.

87. **Rewards Card:** A credit card that rewards spending with points, cash back programs or airline miles. These types of cards usually require that borrowers have good credit and commonly involve an annual fee.

88. **Risk Score:** Another term for a credit score.

89. **Schumer Box:** An easy to use chart that explains the rates, fees, terms and conditions of a credit account. Creditors are required to provide this on credit applications by the U.S. Truth in Lending Act and it usually appears on statements and other documents.

90. **Secured Credit Card:** A consumer credit account that requires the borrower to produce some form of collateral—usually a cash deposit equal to the amount of the credit limit on the card. Secured credit cards are easier to obtain than standard credit accounts and are helpful for borrowers with poor credit or no credit.

91. **Secured Debt:** A loan that requires a piece of property (such as a house or car) to be used as collateral. This collateral provides security for the lender, since the property can be seized and sold if you don't repay the debt.

92. Settlement: An agreement reached with a creditor to pay a debt for less than the total amount due. Settlements can be noted on your credit report and can negatively impact your credit score. The only time it is a good idea to settle a debt is if the debt has already gone to collections or is significantly past due. Settling a debt that is current and in good standing can have a severe negative impact on your credit score.

93. Social Security Number: Also referred to as an SSN. This unique nine digit number is meant to track your Social Security savings but is also used by creditors, lenders, banks, insurers, hospitals, employers and numerous other businesses to identify you and accounts. People who do not have a SSN, such as non-US citizens, use a nine digit Individual Taxpayer Identification Number (ITIN) instead.

94. **Soft Inquiry:** A type of inquiry that does not harm your credit score. Soft inquires are recorded when a business accesses your credit data for a purpose other than an application for credit. Soft inquiries include your request to see your own credit report and employment-related requests. This type of inquiry is recorded by the credit bureaus but does not usually appear on a credit report purchased by you or a business.

95. **Sub-prime Borrower:** A borrower who does not meet the qualifications for standard or "prime" credit and loan offers. Usually a sub-prime borrower has poor credit (a score under 650) due to late payments, collection accounts or public records. Lenders often grade them based on the severity of past credit problems, with categories ranging from "A-" to "D" or lower. Sub-prime borrowers can qualify for loans and credit, but usually at a higher interest rate or with special terms.

96. **Teletrack:** A credit reporting system that specifically tracks subprime borrowers or borrowers with no official credit. Data about payday loan payments, rent payments and non-standard lenders is collected to develop accurate risk predictions for borrowers who may not be included in the standard credit reporting system.

97. **Tradeline:** The official term for an account listed on a credit report. Account details (including payment history, balances, limits and dates) are recorded in a separate tradeline. Tradelines are usually reported to the credit bureaus using an automated "trade tape" system, but in the case of Dun & Bradstreet, tradelines can be reported directly by the consumer, verified and added by Dun & Bradstreet.

98. **Universal Default Clause:** A credit card policy that allows a creditor to increase your interest rates if you make a late payment on any account, not just on their account. Universal default clauses were banned under the CARD Act - credit card issuers are no longer allowed to use this practice to increase cardholder interest rates.

99. **Unsecured Debt:** A loan on which there is no collateral. Most credit card accounts are unsecured debt.

100. **Utilization Ratio:** The ratio between the credit limits on your accounts and the outstanding balances. This ratio shows lenders how much of your available credit you are using overall.

101. **Variable Rate:** A type of adjustable rate loan tied directly to the movement of some other economic index. For example, a variable rate might be prime rate plus 3%; it will adjust as the prime rate does.

Credit and Debt Resource Letters

In the following section you will find several letters that will help you work on improving your credit, settle debts, stop credit harassment and obtain your credit reports. These letters were professionally written and can be very effective if you will use them as instructed. The key to being successful when communicating with creditors and the credit bureaus is to be consistent.

Here is what you can expect:

Scare tactics – You may receive correspondence from the credit bureaus telling you that you may be committing fraud by sending them letters about your credit. Do not fall for this and do not be afraid. The credit improvement process these letters use are completely legal and the credit bureaus must follow the law and respond to your demands.

Stall tactics – If you do not receive a response back from a creditor, collector, or credit bureaus within the timeframes stated in these letters – do not stop the process! Consistency is the key to becoming successful.

The need to be patient – Do not be in a rush to achieve the results you desire. This process takes time but can be effective if you are patient.

Credit Bureau Contact Information

Equifax Credit Information Services, Inc.
P.O. Box 740241
Atlanta, Georgia 30374

1-888-766-0008
www.equifax.com

TransUnion LLC Consumer Disclosure Center
P.O. Box 1000
Chester, Pennsylvania 19022

1-800-888-4213
www.tuc.com

Experian National Consumer Assistance Center
PO Box 2002
Allen, TX 75013

1-888-397-3742
www.experian.com

Amending Previous Payment Agreements with Creditors

Your Name
Home Address
Phone Number

Attention: {name of collector}
Name of Debt Collection
Agency Address

Account Number: {place account or reference number here}

Dear Mr. /Ms. {Creditor}

This letter is to inform you that my financial situation has worsened since our previous payment agreement. Given my significantly reduced income, I have no choice but to request an amendment to our original payment agreement dated {insert date}.

Based on my current income and the number of other creditors I owe, I promise to pay $ _________ each month, (week, every two weeks etc.) until my account is paid in full.

If my financial situation improves and I am able to increase my payment, I will contact you immediately. Please send written confirmation of your acceptance or rejection of this offer to my address outlined above.

As a show of good faith I have enclosed payment in the amount of the lower payment. I thank you for your understanding in this matter and look forward to your favorable consideration. If you have any questions concerning this matter I can be reached at (insert phone number and area code).

Sincerely,

Signature
Printed Name

Letter Closing Inactive Credit Accounts with Zero Balance

Your Name
Home Address
Phone Number

Attention: {Creditor's Name}
Creditor's Address
RE: Account #: {your account number here}

Dear Accounting Department {or Creditor's Name if you have it}

Please close the above referenced account effective immediately. I spoke with {insert name} on {insert date} at {insert time}, and {he/she} assured me that the "payoff balance" would be no more than $ {insert dollar/cents amount}. I've enclosed a check for that exact amount.

Or alternatively... Please close the above referenced account effective immediately. My records indicate the account has a zero balance.

Please send me written confirmation that this account has a zero balance and the date the account was closed . Also, include proof that you've complied with section 623(a)(4) of the Fair Credit Reporting Act by reporting this account as "closed by consumer" to the national credit bureaus.

Thank you for your cooperation. If you have any questions concerning this matter I can be reached at (insert daytime phone number and area code)

Sincerely,

Signature
Printed Name

Disputing Errors on Credit Card Bills

Your Full Name
Current Address
Current Phone Number

Name of Credit Card Company
Mailing Address (Check your statement for the correct address. It's usually different than the one you mail payments too.)
City, State, Zip

Dear {Insert name of Credit Card Company from statement}

I am disputing an item on my statement, dated {insert date of statement}. Please note that this letter is dated within the 60-day limit required under the Fair Credit Billing Act.

or use the following paragraph instead

I am disputing an item on my statement dated {insert date of statement} because I am unable to determine from my records what the charge is for. I need more information about line item {place the line item number or description here}. Please send copies of any documents you have pertaining to this item.

Please use the following information to investigate my claim:

{Insert your name as it appears on your credit card statement}

Date of Statement: {Insert the date from the statement you are disputing}

Account Number: {Insert credit card account number}

Date of Transaction: {Insert date from statement}

Description of Transaction {Copy from statement}

Describe Error: {If disputing dollar amount, insert amount using $0.00 format}

{Insert explanation of why you believe an error occurred} see more examples below

I understand that you have 30 days to respond and 90 days to either resolve my dispute or inform me in writing of why the bill is correct. Until then, I will pay any amount due except for the amount in question and await your letter explaining all actions taken concerning this dispute.

If your investigation shows the information to be accurate, I respectfully request that you provide an explanation of your findings, a statement of what I owe, including any finance charges that have accumulated and any minimum payments I've missed while questioning this bill. If I agree with your findings, you can expect my payment in the amount you say I owe within the 10-day limit allowed under the Fair Credit Billing Act.

Sincerely,

Signature
Printed Name

Confirming Actions Promised by the Company or Creditor

Your Name
Your Address

Business Name
Business Address

Re: (account number, if applicable)

Dear {use the name of the person with whom you spoke with}

Thank you for speaking with me today and for agreeing to resolve my complaint.

For the record, my complaint is (clearly but briefly describe your complaint - use facts)

As agreed upon in our conversation, you will state that you or your company will (state the specific action agreed upon including all details) See note below

Thank you for your help and understanding.

Sincerely,

Signature
Printed Name

Confirming Payment Agreements With Creditors Based On Your Current Financial Hardship

Your Name
Your Address

Attention: {Creditor's Name}
Credit Department
Creditor's Address

RE: Account #: {your account number here}

Dear Mr. /Ms. {insert name of person you spoke with}

Thank you for speaking with me today about my temporary problem in making my normal payments, and for also agreeing to the following payment arrangement on my account.

As agreed upon in our conversation, I will make reduced payments in the amount of $ _____ on or before the ______ of each month for a period of ____ months and after that time will resume making normal payments.

Thank you for your help and understanding in this matter. If you have any questions regarding this matter I can be reached at (insert daytime phone number with area code).

Sincerely,

Signature
Printed Name

Debt Collection Dispute Letter

Your Name
Your Address

Collector's Name
Collector's Address

Dear {insert name of collector or company},

I am writing in response to your (letter or phone call) dated {insert date}, (copy enclosed) because I do not believe I owe what you say I owe.

This is the first I've heard from you, or any other company on this matter therefore, in accordance with the Fair Debt Collection Practices Act, Section 809(b): Validating Debts:

(b) If the consumer notifies the debt collector in writing within the thirty-day period described in subsection (a) that the debt, or any portion thereof, is disputed, or that the consumer requests the name and address of the original creditor, the debt collector shall cease collection of the debt, or any disputed portion thereof, until the debt collector obtains verification of the debt or any copy of a judgment, or the name and address of the original creditor, and a copy of such verification or judgment, or name and address of the original creditor, is mailed to the consumer by the debt collector.

I respectfully request that you provide me with the following information:

*(1) the amount of the debt;
*(2) the name of the creditor to whom the debt is owed;
*(3) Provide a verification or copy of any judgment (if applicable);
*(4) Proof that you are licensed to collect debts in (insert name of your state)

Be advised that I am fully aware of my rights under the Fair Debt Collection Practices Act and the Fair Credit Reporting Act. For instance, I know that:

* because I have disputed this debt in writing within 30 days of receipt of your dunning notice, you must obtain verification of the debt or a copy of the judgment against me and mail these items to me at your expense;

* you cannot add interest or fees except those allowed by the original contract or state law.

* you do not have to respond to this dispute and if you do, any attempt to collect this debt without validating it, violates the FDCPA;

Also be advised that I am keeping very accurate records of all correspondence from you and your company including recording all phone calls and I will not hesitate to report violations of the law to my State Attorney General, the Federal Trade Commission and the Better Business Bureau.

I have disputed this debt; therefore, until validated you know your information concerning this debt is inaccurate. Thus, if you have already reported this debt to any credit-reporting agency (CRA) or Credit Bureau (CB) then, you must immediately inform them of my dispute with this debt. Reporting information that you know to be inaccurate or failing to report information correctly violates the Fair Credit Reporting Act § 1681s-2. Should you pursue a judgment without validating this debt, I will inform the judge and request the case be dismissed based on your failure to comply with the FDCPA.

Finally, if you do not own this debt, I demand that you immediately send a copy of this dispute letter to the original creditor so they are also aware of my dispute with this debt.

Signature
Printed Name

Follow Up Debt Collection Dispute Letter - Same Collector

Your Name
Your Address

Collector's Name
Collector's Address

Dear Collector,

I am writing in response to your {letter or phone call} dated {insert date of letter or phone call}, copy enclosed.

On {insert date of initial dispute letter} I sent you a letter explaining that I do not believe I owe what you say I owe and, in accordance with the Fair Debt Collection Practices Act, 15 USC 1692g, Section 809(b): Validating Debts:

(b) If the consumer notifies the debt collector in writing within the thirty-day period described in subsection (a) that the debt, or any portion thereof, is disputed, or that the consumer requests the name and address of the original creditor, the debt collector shall cease collection of the debt, or any disputed portion thereof, until the debt collector obtains verification of the debt or any copy of a judgment, or the name and address of the original creditor, and a copy of such verification or judgment, or name and address of the original creditor, is mailed to the consumer by the debt collector.

I must remind you that in my previous letter I requested the following information:

*(1) the amount of the debt;
*(2) the name of the original creditor to whom the debt is owed;
*(3) Provide a verification or copy of any judgment (if applicable);

*(4) Proof that you are licensed to collect debts in (insert name of your state)

I also requested that if you have reported me to any credit reporting agency, that you inform them that I have placed this debt in dispute and to provide me with proof that you have done so. Furthermore, I asked that you immediately send a copy of that dispute letter to the company (creditor) that you say I owe money to, so they are also aware of my dispute with this debt.

As of today, you have failed to respond to my requests! For your convenience, I have included a copy of my previous letter and a copy of the mail receipt showing that you received my letter on {insert date from mail receipt}.

Since you have failed to respond, I assume that you have been unable to validate the debt and therefore, I consider this matter closed. You may consider this letter your official notification that I do not intend to correspond with you on this matter again unless you comply with my requests, the FDCPA and the FCRA.

I must remind you that any attempt to collect this debt without validating it, violates the FDCPA and that I am recording all phone calls and keeping all correspondence concerning this matter. Be advised that I will not hesitate to report violations of the law to my State Attorney General, the Federal Trade Commission and the national Better Business Bureau.

Signature
Printed Name

Dispute Debt Collection with a New Collection Agency

Your Name
Home Address
Phone Number

Attention: {name of creditor or collector}
Name of Agency
Agency Address

Account Number: {account or reference number}

Dear Mr. /Ms.

I am writing in response to your (letter or phone call) dated {insert date}, (copy enclosed) because I do not believe I owe what you say I owe.

This is the (insert proper number) time I've disputed this debt. The first dispute was on {insert date} with {insert name of collection agency} and the second was on {insert date} with {insert name of collection agency}. Be advised that neither collection agency responded to my dispute.

In accordance with the Fair Debt Collection Practices Act, Section 809(b): Validating Debts:

(b) If the consumer notifies the debt collector in writing within the thirty-day period described in subsection (a) that the debt, or any portion thereof, is disputed, or that the consumer requests the name and address of the original creditor, the debt collector shall cease collection of the debt, or any disputed portion thereof, until the debt collector obtains verification of the debt or any copy of a judgment, or the name and address of the original creditor, and a copy of such verification or judgment, or name and address of the original creditor, is mailed to the consumer by the debt collector.

I respectfully request that you provide me with the following information:

* (1) the amount of the debt;
* (2) the name of the creditor to whom the debt is owed;
* (3) Provide a verification or copy of any judgment (if applicable);
* (4) Proof that you are licensed to collect debts in (insert name of your state)

Be advised that I am fully aware of my rights under the Fair Debt Collection Practices Act and the Fair Credit Reporting Act. For instance, I know that:

* because I have disputed this debt in writing within 30 days of receipt of your dunning notice, you must obtain verification of the debt or a copy of the judgment against me and mail these items to me at your expense;
* you cannot add interest or fees accept those allowed by the original contract or state law.
* you do not have to respond to this dispute but if you do, any attempt to collect this debt without validating it, violates the FDCPA;

Be advised that I am keeping very accurate records of all correspondence from you and your company including recording all phone calls and I will not hesitate to report violations of the law to my State Attorney General, the Federal Trade Commission and the Better Business Bureau.

I have disputed this debt; therefore, until validated you know your information concerning this debt is inaccurate. Thus, if you have already reported this debt to any credit-reporting agency (CRA) or Credit Bureau (CB) then, you must immediately inform them of my dispute with this debt. Reporting information that you know to be inaccurate or failing to report information correctly violates the Fair Credit Reporting Act § 1681s-2. Should you pursue a judgment without validating this debt, I will inform the judge and request the case be dismissed based on your failure to comply with the FDCPA.

If you do NOT own the rights to collect this debt, I demand that you immediately send a copy of this dispute letter to the original creditor that you say I owe money too so they are also aware of my dispute with this debt.

Signature
Printed Name

Disputing Debts that You Believe are Still Invalid

Your Name
Home Address
Phone Number

Attention: {name of collector}
Name of Agency
Agency Address

Account Number: {account or reference number}

Dear Mr. /Ms.

This letter is to inform you that I still dispute this debt. After receiving your response to my original dispute letter, I contacted the original creditor who was unable to verify this account as mine.

In my opinion, you have failed to validate this debt. I must remind you that I originally disputed this debt within the 30-day dispute period outlined in the FDCPA and that I am now also responding in a timely manner to your attempt to validate this debt. Because I still consider this debt as "still in dispute" I do not expect to hear from you again except to provide information or documentation to clear up my reasons for disputing this debt.

I already advised you in my previous letter that I am fully aware of my rights under the Fair Debt Collection Practices Act and the Fair Credit Reporting Act and that I will not hesitate to take all legal steps necessary to protect myself. Be advised that I am keeping accurate records of all correspondence including tape recording all phone calls.

Signature
Printed Name

Debt Payment Agreement Letter

Your Name
Your Address

Attention: {name of collector}
Name of Debt Collection Agency
Address

RE: Your {letter dated} or {phone call on date} reference account #: {place account or reference number here}

Dear Mr. /Ms. {Collector's Name}

According to my records and your {phone call or letter} the balance of this debt is $_____. I am not disputing this debt however; my current financial situation prohibits me from paying the amount you're demanding. I am able to make payments on this account every {insert date of month} to your company in the amount of $ _________.

I would appreciate a call from you confirming your acceptance of my payment terms. However, if I do not hear from you, I will consider your cashing or depositing my check as confirmation that you accept my payment terms. If you do not accept my terms then I expect the enclosed payment to be returned to me immediately in the enclosed self-addressed stamped envelop.

As a show of good faith I've enclosed my first payment in the amount of $________. If my financial situation improves enough for me to increase my payment amount I will contact you immediately. Thank you for understanding.

Sincerely,

Signature
Your Printed Name

Debt Settlement Offer Letter

Your Name
Home Address
Phone Number

Attention: {name of collector or collection agency}
Address

RE: Collection letter dated {date of letter here} or phone call on {date of call here} reference account #: {account or reference number}

Dear Mr./Ms. {Collector's or Collection Agency's Name}

I do not agree that I owe as much as you claim I owe on the above referenced account. In an effort to save both of us a great deal of time and expense I am offering to settle this account for $ ________.

If you accept my offer, please send written confirmation to my address listed above. Once I receive your written confirmation, I will mail payment to your organization within five business days. If you wish to discuss this settlement offer, I can be reached at (insert daytime phone number with area code). However, please understand that I will not make any payment until receiving written confirmation that you accept my offer.

Sincerely,

Signature
Your Printed Name

Final Payment Warning Letter

Your Name
Home Address
Phone Number

Attention: {name of creditor or collector}
Name of Agency
Agency Address

Account Number: {account or reference number}

Dear Mr. /Ms.

My records show the balance on the above referenced account to be $_______. This letter is to inform you that in 30 days from the date of this letter I intend to send a final payment for that exact amount and mark the instrument "Paid in Full".

If you disagree with my calculations, I expect to receive a written explanation from you before 30 days otherwise I will assume you agree with my calculations and will accept my final payment and, after cashing my final payment show my account as zero balance.

If you have any questions concerning this matter, I can be reached at {insert daytime phone number and area code}.

Sincerely,

Signature
Your Printed Name

Judgment Proof Notification Letter

Your Name
Your Address

Collector' or Creditor Name
Address

RE: Account {insert account name and/or number}

Dear Collector or Creditor,

I am writing in response to your (letter or phone call) dated {insert date}, (copy enclosed) about the above referenced account. I am unable to pay on this account due to {insert reason here i.e. unemployed, disability}. This is a {permanent or temporary} situation.

I also hope to save both of us a great deal of time, energy and expense by letting you know that I have no attachable income or own any assets such as a home, car or land; essentially I have no money and can prove it! In accordance with the Fair Debt Collection Practices Act, 15 USC 1692c, 805(c):

(c) CEASING COMMUNICATION. "If a consumer notifies a debt collector in writing that the consumer refuses to pay a debt or that the consumer wishes the debt collector to cease further communication with the consumer, the debt collector shall not communicate further with the consumer with respect to such debt..."

Although I agree that I owe this debt, I am unable to make any payments toward it and therefore ask that you cease further communication with me concerning this debt. I will notify you if my financial situation improves enough to allow me to begin or resume making payments. Thank you for your understanding in this matter.

Signature
Printed Name

Paid in Full - Informing Collectors of Your Final Payment

Your Name
Home Address
Phone Number

Attention: {name of collector}
Name of Debt Collection
Agency Address

Account Number: {account or reference number}

Dear Mr. /Ms. {Collector's Name or Collection Agency's name}

You'll find my final payment on the above referenced account enclosed. I request written confirmation showing this account as {paid in full or settled} according to our agreement on {insert date of agreement}. However, should you choose not you provide me with confirmation, I will use your acceptance of this final payment as proof that you agree the account is {paid in full or settled}.

Now that this debt is paid, I do not expect to hear from you except to confirm the account is paid. I will consider any other contact from you or you company as harassment and will immediately report your actions to my State Attorney General and to the Federal Trade Commission and, if necessary, take whatever legal action is necessary to protect myself. Finally, I expect you to remove this account and all references to my personal information from your records.

Signature
Your Printed Name

Payment Refusal and Termination Letter

Your Name
Home Address
Phone Number

Attention: {name of creditor or collector}
Name of Agency
Agency Address
Account Number: {account or reference number}

Dear Mr. /Ms. {Collector's Name}

I have paid on this account per our payment agreement dated (insert date of verbal or written agreement). My records indicate that I have made (insert number) payments in the amount(s) of $(insert amount(s) for a total of $(insert total) in payments leaving a balance of $(insert balance).

Although I certainly want to continue paying on this debt, I simply cannot afford to pay the amount you are now demanding so, per your (phone call or letter) informing me that you refuse to accept my payments, you leave me no choice but to terminate our relationship.

For the record, do not contact me again regarding this account unless it is to inform me that my previous payment offer is acceptable or that you intend to take other actions as outlined in the Fair Debt Collection Practice Act.

Should you decide that some type of legal action is necessary, be advised that I welcome the opportunity to show any judge my efforts to resolve this issue. I have kept extremely accurate records of all correspondence and payments, and therefore, have complete confidence that any court would agree that my efforts have been in good faith.

Signature
Your Printed Name

Previously Settled Debt Letter

Your Name
Home Address
Phone Number

Attention: {name of collector if known}
Name of Debt Collection Agency
Address

RE: Collection letter dated {date of letter here} or phone call on {date of call here} reference account #: {account or reference number}

Dear Mr. /Ms. {Collector's Name of name of Collection Agency}

This letter is to inform you that the account in question was settled on [insert date] with [insert name of collection agency]. I have enclosed copies of the settlement letter and proof of payment. You now have proof that this debt is no longer collectable, therefore I demand that you remove this account, and all references to my personal information, from your records.

I do not expect to hear from you again regarding this matter however, should you choose to ignore this notification, I will consider any contact not in accordance with the Fair Debt Collection Act, a serious violation of the law and will immediately report any violations to my State Attorney General and to the Federal Trade Commission and, should it become necessary, take legal action to protect my myself.

Signature
Your Printed Name

Expired Statute of Limitations Notification Letter

Your Name
Your Address

Collector's Name
Collector's Address

RE: [insert account number or name of account or name of debt]:

Dear [insert collector's name or company name],

This letter is in response to your [letter dated xx-xx-2005] (copy enclosed) or [phone call on xx-xx-2005], concerning the collection of the above referenced [account or date].

I do not believe I owe what you say I owe therefore I dispute this debt. I am well aware of my rights under the Fair Debt Collection Practices Act (FDCPA) and my state laws so I hope to save both of us a great deal of time by letting you know that not only do I dispute the validity of this debt, I have also checked with my State Attorney General and verified that the Statute of Limitations for enforcing this type of debt through the courts in (insert your state or the state in which the contract was signed) has expired. Therefore, should you decide to pursue this matter in court I intend to inform the court of my dispute of this debt and that the "statute of limitations" has expired.

This letter is your formal notification that I consider this matter closed and demand that you, or anyone affiliated with your company, stop contacting me regarding this or any other matter except to advise me that your debt collection efforts are being terminated or that you or the creditor are taking specific actions allowed by the FDCPA or my state laws.

Be advised that I consider any contact not in accordance with the Fair Debt Collection Practices Act a serious violation of the law and will immediately report any violations to my State Attorney General, to the Federal Trade Commission and, if necessary, take whatever legal action is necessary to protect myself. Be advised that I tape record all phone calls and violations of the FDCPA can result in you or your company being personally fined up to $1,000 per incident.

Signature
Printed Name

Stop Debt Collection Calls

Your Name
Your Address

Collector's Name
Collector's Address

Mr./Ms. Collector,

I am writing in response to your constant phone calls!

According to the Fair Debt Collection Practices Act, [15 USC 1692c] Section 805(c): CEASING COMMUNICATION: You must cease all communication with me after being notified in writing that I no longer wish to communicate with you. Therefore, I demand that you stop calling me at home, at work, on my cell phone or at any other location!

In accordance with the federal FDCPA, now that you have received this "stop calling" letter, you may only contact me to inform me that you:

* are terminating further collection efforts;
* invoking specified remedies which are ordinarily invoked by you or your company; or
* intend to invoke a specified remedy.

Be advised that I am well aware of my rights! For instance, I know that any future contact by you or your company violates the FDCPA and that since you already have my location information, calls made by you or your company to any 3rd party concerning me violates section 805(b)2 of the FDCPA.

Be advised that I am keeping accurate records of all correspondence from you and your company, including tape recording all phone calls. If you continue calling me I will pursue all available legal actions to stop you from harassing me and my family.

Signature
Printed Name

Debt Validation Letter

Your Name
Address

Collector's Name
Collector's address

Re: Acct # XXXX-XXXX-XXXX-XXXX

Dear Collector:

This letter is being sent to you in response to a notice sent to me on (insert date letter sent by collector). Be advised that this is not a refusal to pay, but a notice sent pursuant to the Fair Debt Collection Practices Act, 15 USC 1692(g) that your claim is disputed and validation is requested.

This is NOT a request for "verification" or proof of my mailing address, but a request for VALIDATION made pursuant to the above named title and section. I respectfully request that your offices provide me with competent evidence that I have any legal obligation to pay you.

Please provide me with the following: a simple accounting of the debt, the name and address of the original creditor, and the original account number. Also, please show me that you are licensed to collect in my state and provide me with your license numbers and your Registered Agent.

Your anticipated cooperation in this regard is greatly appreciated.

Best Regards,

Signature
Printed Name

Correct Inaccurate information in Your Personal Credit Profiles

Your Full Name
Current Address
Current Phone Number

Attention: {insert credit reporting agency name}
{add CRA address here}

Dear {credit reporting agency}

This letter is a formal request to correct inaccurate information contained in my credit file. The item(s) listed below is/are completely (insert appropriate word(s) {inaccurate, incorrect, incomplete, erroneous, misleading, outdated}). I have enclosed a copy of the credit report your organization provided to me on {insert date of report here} and circled in red the item(s) in question.

Line Item: {insert name of creditor, account number or line item number)

Item Description: (this info is found on your credit report)

Requested Correction: (describe exactly what you want. If you want an item deleted say so and explain why. If you want an item corrected or updated, provide the correct information such as names, dates, amounts and so forth and any evidence to support your claim).

In accordance with the federal Fair Credit Reporting Act (FCRA), I respectfully request you investigate my claim and, if after your investigation, you find my claim to be valid and accurate, I request that you immediately {delete, update, correct} the item.

Furthermore, I request that you supply a corrected copy of my credit profile to me and all creditors who have received a copy within the last 6 months, or the last 2 years for employment purposes. Additionally, please provide me with the name, address, and telephone number of each credit grantor or other subscriber that you provided a copy of my credit report too within the past six months.

If your investigation shows the information to be accurate, I respectfully request that you forward to me a description of the procedure used to determine the accuracy and completeness of the item in question within 15 days of the completion of your re-investigation as required by the Fair Credit Reporting Act.

I thank you for your consideration and cooperation. If you have any questions concerning this matter I can be reached at (insert daytime phone number including area code).

Sincerely,

Signature
Printed Name

Follow-up Dispute Letter for Correcting Personal Credit Reports

Full Name
Current Address
Current Phone Number

Attention: {insert credit reporting agency name}
{add CRA address here}

RE: Dispute Letter Dated {place the date of your initial letter here}

Dear {credit reporting agency}

This letter is a formal notice that you have failed to respond in a timely manner to my letter dated, {place the date of your initial letter here}, and deposited by registered mail with the Post Office on that date. For your benefit, and as a gesture of my goodwill, I will restate my dispute:

Line Item: {insert name of creditor, account number or line item number}

Item description: (found on your credit report)

The item: is completely (insert appropriate word: inaccurate, incorrect, incomplete, erroneous, misleading, outdated) and needs to be corrected immediately. I have enclosed a copy of your organization's credit report dated {insert date of report here} and for your convenience, circled the item described above.

The Fair Credit Reporting Act requires you to investigate and respond to my dispute within 30 days, yet you have failed to do so. I feel it necessary to remind you that you may be liable for your willful non-compliance and that I am maintaining a careful record of my communications with you on this matter, in case your continued non-compliance forces me to file a complaint with the FTC. (See Title 15 USC 41)

Please do not delay further! {insert the appropriate word here} (Delete, Update, Correct) the information identified above and send corrected credit profile to me and to all creditors who have received a copy within the last 6 months, and the last 2 years for employment purposes.

If your re-investigation was negative, please supply the description of the procedure used to determine the accuracy and completeness of the information to my address listed above.

Sincerely,

Signature
Printed Name

Add 100-Word Statement to Explain Misleading Information in Your Credit Reports

Your Name
Your Address

Attention: {insert credit reporting agency name}
Click for Equifax, Experian or Trans Union Address
{add CRA address here}

Dear {credit reporting agency}

In accordance with the Fair Credit Reporting Act (FCRA), I wish to add a short statement to my credit file explaining information that your reinvestigation failed to resolve to my satisfaction. For your convenience, I've quoted the specific paragraph from the FCRA that gives me the right to add this statement to my credit file:

Section 611b. Statement of Dispute: "If the reinvestigation does not resolve the dispute, the consumer may file a brief statement setting forth the nature of the dispute. The consumer reporting agency may limit such statements to not more than one hundred words if it provides the consumer with assistance in writing a clear summary of the dispute."

Therefore, in reference to the following line item:

{Place name of creditor here}

{Place account number and/or line item number here}

Please add the following statement to my credit file

"On September 20, I was called up to active duty and sent on a 179 day overseas deployment. During this time my active duty pay was significantly less than my civilian pay causing me a great deal of financial hardship and making it nearly impossible for me to pay all of my debts. Please note that within a very short period of time (120 days) of my release from active duty I brought this account current. The problem is now resolved and will not affect my finances." Click here for additional statement suggestions

Please provide me written confirmation that you have added the above statement to my credit file within 30 days of this request.

Sincerely,

Signature
Printed Name

Have Outdated Information Removed from Personal Credit Reports, Credit Profiles and Credit History

Your Full Name
Current Address
Current Phone Number

Attention: {insert credit reporting agency name}
Click for Equifax, Experian or Trans Union Address
{add CRA address here}

Dear {credit reporting agency}

This letter is a formal request to remove outdated information from my credit report. For easy reference, I've enclosed a copy of the credit report that your organization provided me on {insert date of report} with the outdated items circled in red. I've also listed the items below:

Line Item {insert number}:

insert name and date of item}

In accordance with the Fair Credit Reporting Act, Section 605 [15 U.S.C. § 1681c] "Running of Reporting Period", as of December 29, 1997, reporting periods only run 7 or 10 years depending on the type of information. In my case, the information in question expired as of [insert date].

I respectfully ask you to investigate my claim and if you find my claim to be valid then I expect you to immediately remove the outdated items identified in this letter and any additional outdated items that you discover during your investigation. Furthermore, after correcting my credit file, I request that you forward a corrected copy of my credit report to me at the address listed at the top of this letter.

Finally, if your investigation determines the information is not outdated, I respectfully request you forward to me a description of the procedure used to determine the accuracy and completeness of the item in question. In accordance with the FCRA I respectfully request you forward this information within 15 days of the completion of your re-investigation.

Thank you for your consideration and cooperation in resolving this matter. If you have any questions concerning this issue I can be reached at: {insert daytime phone number including area code).

Sincerely,

Signature
Printed Name

Get Unauthorized Hard Credit Inquiries Removed from Your Personal Credit Reports

Your Full Name
Current Address
Current Phone Number

Attention: {Creditor's Name}
Credit Department
Creditor's Address

Dear {Creditor's Name}

This letter is your formal notice to cease your unauthorized hard inquiries into my credit report and, a formal demand that you immediately contact the credit reporting agencies and credit bureaus, where your organization has made inquiries into my credit history, to have your illegal inquiries removed. Be advised that I will be checking my reports to ensure you have had the following unauthorized inquiries removed:

Line Item {insert number}:

Made by: {insert name of company or person making the inquiry

Made on: {insert date of inquiry}

Made with: {insert name of credit reporting agency}

To my knowledge, I have not signed any documents authorizing your organization to view my credit history therefore, your inquiry into my credit report violates the Fair Credit Reporting Act, Section 1681b(c): Transactions Not Initiated by Consumer.

If you are in possession of any document that you believe authorizes you or your organization to make inquires into my credit report, I respectfully request a copy of this document be sent to my address listed above so that I may verify its validity. Given the amount of identity theft, I'm sure you'll agree that verifying your information is in your best interest.

Finally, assuming you do not posses inquiry authorization, I request that, after removing your unauthorized inquires from my credit profiles, you also remove all of my personal information from your records and send me confirmation that you have complied with my requests.

Sincerely,

Signature
Printed Name

Get Unauthorized Credit Inquiries Removed

Your Full Name
Current Address
Current Phone Number

Attention: {insert credit reporting agency name} See names and addresses below
{add CRA address here}

Dear {credit reporting agency}

This letter is a formal request to remove unauthorized inquiries from my credit report. I've enclosed a copy of the credit report that your organization provided me on {insert date of report}. I've listed the unauthorized inquiries below and also circled them in red on the enclosed report

Line Item {insert number}:

Creditor: {insert name of creditor(s) making the inquiry}

Please note that before making this request, I sent letters to the organizations responsible for these unauthorized inquires asking them to remove their inquiries from my credit reports and to cease their illegal activity. Although I sent these letters return receipt requested and have proof that my letters were received more than 30 days ago, they have failed to respond therefore, I ask for your assistance in resolving this matter.

In accordance with the Fair Credit Reporting Act, I respectfully ask you to investigate my claim and, if after your investigation, you find my claim to be valid and accurate, I ask that you immediately delete the unauthorized inquiries outlined below. Furthermore, I ask that you send a corrected copy of my credit profile to me at the above address.

If your investigation determines the inquiry was authorized, I respectfully request you forward to me a description of the procedure used to determine this within 15 days of the completion of your re-investigation.

Thank you for your consideration and cooperation and if you have any questions concerning this matter I can be reached at (insert daytime phone number including area code).

Sincerely,

Signature
Printed Name

Notice to File an FTC Complaint

Your Name
Your Address

Name of Credit Bureau See addresses below
Credit Bureau's Address

Dear Credit Bureau,

RE: Dispute Letter dated {date of initial letter}, and Follow-up Letter dated {date of second letter}

NOTICE OF INTENT TO FILE FORMAL FTC COMPLAINT

This letter shall serve as formal notice of my intent to file a complaint with the Federal Trade Commission (FTC), due to your failure to respond to my two previous letters requesting a correction to my credit file.

As indicated by the enclosed copies of letters and mailing receipts, you have received from me by registered mail, a dispute letter dated {date of initial letter}, as well as a follow-up letter, dated {date of second letter}.

I am sure that you are aware of the Fair Credit Reporting Act's requirement to respond to consumer's credit report disputes within 30 days, and that the FTC investigates complaints for failure to respond. I have advised you on two separate occasions, more than 75 days ago and again 40 days ago that you are reporting inaccurate information about me. For the record and your benefit, I will restate my dispute:

Line Item: {insert name of creditor, account number or line item number)

Item Description: (this info is found on your credit report)

Requested Correction: (describe exactly what you want. If you want an item deleted say so and explain why. If you want an item corrected or updated, provide the correct information such as names, dates, amounts and so forth and any evidence to support your claim).

“The item above is completely (insert appropriate word: inaccurate, incorrect, incomplete, erroneous, misleading, outdated) and needs to be corrected immediately. I have enclosed a copy of your organization’s credit report dated {insert date of report here} and for your convenience, circled the item(s) described above.

If you do not immediately take steps to resolve this issue, I will be forced to file a formal complaint with the FTC. Furthermore, I intend to consider seeking redress in civil court to recover damages, costs, and attorney fees, should you fail to respond.

Furthermore I expect you to supply me with a description of the procedure used to determine the accuracy and completeness of the disputed information, provide a corrected credit profile to me, all creditors who have received a copy within the last 6 months, and the last 2 years for employment purposes and the name, address, and telephone number of each credit grantor or other subscriber who have received a copy of my credit profile within the last 6 months.

If your re-investigation was negative, please supply the description of the procedure used to determine the accuracy and completeness of the information to my address above. If you have any questions concerning this matter I can be reached at (insert daytime phone number including area code).

Sincerely,

Signature
Printed Name

Requesting Free Credit Reports

Full Name
Current Address
Current Phone Number

Name and Address National Credit Bureaus Contact Information
of National Credit Bureau

Dear Credit Bureau,

I am requesting a free copy of my credit report from your organization in accordance with the Fair Credit Reporting Act, Section 1681j (b) and (c). My qualifying reason(s) is/are (insert one or more of the qualifying reasons from above)

For example: On {insert date here} I was refused credit by {name of creditor}. I've enclosed a copy of the creditor's refusal letter.

Please use the following personal information to locate and forward the report to me:

Full Legal Name: {insert your full name}
Birthday: {insert your birth date in this format mm/dd/yyyy
Social Security Number: {insert your 9-digit number}
Current Address: {insert your complete address}
Former Address: {insert previous addresses if you have moved more than once in the last five years)

I've also enclosed copies of my driver's license, {or utility bill} showing my current address, and a photocopy of my Social Security card. Please do not share my information with any other agency. I look forward to your speedy reply and if you have any questions concerning this request I can be reached at {insert daytime phone number and area code). Thank you.

Order Form
and
Contact Information

To order by mail, fill out this form and send it along with your check or money order to:

Worthingham Publishing
8306 Wilshire Blvd. Suite 303
Beverly Hills, Ca. 90211

Cost per copy $19.99 plus $3.50 P&H

Ship ______ copies of Situations 101 Relationships

Ship ______ copies of Situations 101 Finances

to

Name: ____________________________________

Address: __________________________________

City, State, Zip ____________________________

To order the Capital Credit xp:
Personal Credit Improvement Software or
The Business Credit Blueprint
log onto
http://www.imagineinternational.biz/goodtimesthelma

Bern Nadette Stanis
contact information:

goodtimesthelma@aol.com

The Worthingham Group
8306 Wilshire Blvd. Suite 303
Beverly Hills, California 90211

Trent T. Daniel
contact information:

tdaniel@situations101.com

The Daniel-Melton Media Group
17117 Westheimer Road Suite 75
Houston, Texas 77082